PRAISE FOᴋ
"FROM CONFLICT TO COMMUNICATION"

"*From Conflict to Communication* is written from the author's personal life experiences, observations of conflict within relationships and politics, and most importantly, from the insights gained from her therapy practice. **Byrne's message is clear: We need Dialogue more than ever in our world today to heal our increasing global culture of confrontation, war, and relational conflict.**"

– Linda Ellinor,
co-author of *Dialogue: Rediscover the Transforming Power of Conversation*, now translated into six languages

"**[Katy Byrne's] lifelong writing about how we can communicate instead of continue our warlike behavior is an important read and contribution to us all.**"

– David Brigode, Affordable Housing Developer and Community Advocate, SF, Bay Area

"Katy Byrne lays out **a positive and important strategy to confront important issues** . . . and hard to manage conversations . . . If you are looking for **tools and approaches [to] help you manage emotional minefields**, this book may help you better understand the psychological dynamics at work."

– Raymond Baltar, Environmental Project Manager

from CONFLICT to
COMMUNICATION

Lessons from Life and my Therapy Office

Katy Byrne, LMFT, MA

From Conflict to Communication:
Lessons from Life and my Therapy Office
by Katy Byrne, LMFT, MA

Copyright © 2024. All rights reserved.
First Printing May 2024

ISBN: 979-8-9904697-0-9 (pbk); 979-8-9904697-1-6 (ebk)

Thank you for buying an authorized edition of this book.

Cover art; cover and interior design by Suzanne Parrott
Interior cartoons by Steve Klein

KB Press
Printed and bound
in the United States of America.

ConversationsWithKaty.com

This writing is dedicated to my community –

no matter how near or far –

you know who you are.

You prop me up when I am discouraged,

you lift me up when I'm scared.

I can't possibly thank you enough.

And to the voiceless ones –

the animals of this world.

Contents

PREFACE

Being honest and real is scary. That's why we don't do it. What we get instead is separation and conflict. In this writing I'm waving my arms wildly saying, "Stop rupturing relationships and start repairing them – personally and politically" – before it's too late.

If we can't co-exist and sustain important dialogues, how can we create a different globe? If we won't talk to each other, work things out, hear each other, and resolve differences, where does that leave us? Fractured, fighting, and at war everywhere, even in our homes and communities.

It's no small goal. How to get this gargantuan globe shaped into a calm, satisfied round ball? Even while I'm writing this with coffee brewing in my kitchen, its delicious, distinctive aroma distracts me from these huge concerns. Then, suddenly, I get a text saying that in our small, sweet town of Sonoma, California, there is a high school "lock down." My heart thumps like a big Taiko drum. What could this mean? School shootings are happening all over the country. While I look at my writing on ending conflict – it contrasts painfully with increasing crime and terrorism. I dive back into this topic

– human rage. I recall reading about our history of horror, including a tribe of people hacking babies heads off that allegedly happened this month in the middle east. How can this kind of cruel anger exist?

At present, we use battles, band-aids, arguments, regulations, prisons, rules, taxes, blame, denial, compartmentalization, etc. They're not helping enough.

The container I create for my therapy clients has taught me what works. *How do you heal a cut?* By airing it. We could have crucial conversations instead. If we support a "holding" – a scaffolding that makes difficult dialogues safe, that's the cure. One of my clients calls them "rules for war." So, *I am absolutely sure resolution of conflict occurs – because I see it every day. When clients quit fighting, it is because they get to the heart of the conflict. They really, really listened to each other and identified their fears, hurt, and needs. They experienced dialogue with dignity, not debate.*

The power of dialogue is what keeps us in circulation with one another.

Forty years of being a psychotherapist and life itself has shown me that repair of conflict is completely possible with a few simple tools. We don't need division, war, fighting, walls, armor, anger, and prejudice running our world. We do desperately need to pledge loyalty to life, the earth, to nature, and to a declaration of interdependence, not the pathology of domination, privilege, tearing down, and destruction.

What shifts arguments to productive dialogue? Being "heard" helps clients explore their emotions and wounds. As long as I carefully guarded the space so that it remained respectful – it was *"half the battle."* It's not always easy. It sounds a lot simpler than it is. I tell my clients it's like lifting weights at the gym. If you're out of shape, it takes time, so does learning to listen well. You feel better and stronger once you're in the new habit. You don't change overnight, but when you do, you feel more vital and alive.

Could countries, politicians, far right and left thinkers, or enraged people stop polarizing and fighting as they experience the power of dialogue? It happens in my office, why not elsewhere? We counselors call this a "parallel process."

As Wendell Berry, the famous environmental activist, said when Amanda Petrusish commented to him in an interview, "The idea of conversation seems important to you." He responded, "It's either that or kill each other." (*The New Yorker*, July 14, 2019.) We're more accustomed to anger and debate, not curiosity and conversation.

If we deepen to the heart of what matters, we'll find a way out of arguments.

The power of dialogue is what keeps us in circulation with one another instead of rigidified and cut off. We aren't helpless against corruption if we stay connected, "of the people, by the people, for the people . . . " (Abraham Lincoln.) The power of dialogue is people power, a way out of arguments. The old way hasn't worked. As Berry said, "our dominant practice now is to solve problems with other problems."

It's time for a new paradigm.

This book poured out of me during the worldwide pandemic. In isolation, I tunneled into a review of my life and what I had learned or still struggled with. My mother's suicide was a gut punch to everything I trusted before that. That unbearable loss showed me how important closure and real conversation are. There will be other stories, including moments when I had a palpable experience of the unified field – the interconnection of the universe. It renewed my belief that we are here to evolve as a species beyond separation.

It is my conviction that conversation can change the world.

I hope that my true stories, the lessons I have learned in life and in my therapy practice, theories, and real experiences demonstrate why dialogue or the absence of it – either makes diplomatic, deep-felt connections happen or leaves us with unnecessary losses.

As Paula Marantz Cohen writes in *Talking Cure: An Essay on the Civilizing Power of Conversation* (The New Yorker Hua Hsu, 3/20/23 *Good Talk*), "Our society abounds in bad conversation," in part because "people would rather regurgitate predetermined positions," she fears, rather than wrestle with ambiguity. "No spaces seem safe for the frictions or disagreements that make conversations go." This gives credence to my experience. Create a milieu for people to be heard, and then solutions and resolutions unfold. *It is my conviction that conversation can change the world.*

What I have learned is that our fight-or-flight instincts – from the amygdala brain and trauma history are deeply implanted in humanity from our childhoods and multi-generations. *We witness destructive, domineering personalities, leaders, or corporate systems and internalize those models – we believe that is what "authority does."* We just "go along" or diss-associate, continuing habits like judging, separating, and colluding with a dysfunctional narrative. (Judging is not discerning; it is meant here as criticism.) We keep blaming and battling. As Terry Patten wrote: " . . . we're in a race between consciousness and catastrophe." He elaborates, "Instead of changing the world, many of us simply change the subject. After all, if we can't actually improve our situations, what's the point of getting worked up? Both reflexive optimism and learned helplessness are based on deep-rooted cultural agreements as well as subtle but very effective personal indoctrination." (*A New Republic of the Heart*)

When clients feel safe, they move from gridlock and go "down the ladder" into feelings or ideas inside. They discover blocks to connection, old beliefs that short-circuited their ability to care, cemented their attitudes and habitual behaviors. Maybe a man is often angry or shut down with his wife,

> *"We're in a race between consciousness and catastrophe."*
> – Terry Patten

unknowingly, because that's how his dad treated his mother. It's "how guys express themselves," he says. It's been normalized. A woman might have learned despair or criticism instead of asking for what she wants, etc.

But, within a protective container, people can unwind the ball of yarn that has gotten tangled inside or between themselves. Sometimes, I think of it as "rocking the baby." We all need protection when scared. I see how much it surprises people to uncover their unconscious, frozen feelings and experience a new way to behave instead. A safe space allows them to explore their insides. "Clearly, the capacity for denial of both external reality and emotion developed in childhood continues into adulthood. The implications for politics are that adults, both ordinary citizens and political leaders, simply deny threatening aspects of reality" or numb their feelings. "However, the problem with denial is that it delays recognition of a problem or a crisis until it becomes severe; even when the facts are indisputable, the denial of feelings reduces empathy for the suffering of others – thereby eliminating an important motivation for addressing the problem." (*Raised to Rage*, Milburn, Conrad)

We can stop prejudice, killing, maiming, genocides, and gaping gaps between the rich and poor. But, we'll have to stare at the seeds of uncivil destruction. I see it daily in my therapy practice. History keeps repeating itself, like invasive weeds returning each spring, even through cracks in the cement. Weed killer isn't working.

What to do about it before we blow ourselves up? We need a way out of this repetition compulsion. What I witness is that certain tools and "guardrails" ensure that each person is seen and heard. They're a safety net for crucial conversations. The diagram for dialogue and a few simple tools are at the back of the book. As we lubricate communication, we can create cooperation in Congress, between countries, schools, neighborhoods, the workplace, courtrooms, prisons, between groups, and in relationships.

My passion for finding a way out of conflict began probably from birth. I was born near the time the holocaust ended. Of course, the atrocity was never spoken about in my family, but I believe it stayed lodged in my memory from the womb.

Then, growing up with an enraged mother whom I adored half of the time when she wasn't yelling in her Jekyll-Hyde swings, I was inevitably drawn to becoming a psychotherapist. When my mother killed herself I woke up to the importance of communication and the losses when we don't. Why hadn't either of us ever felt heard? Since then, no other question has seemed so urgent: *how can we shift from conflict to reparative conversations?*

This writing also started percolating in me as I watched the hope of my generation plummeting into a quagmire of agonizing problems. Then, seeing inspiration in the '60s, our spirits soaring – we were uplifted by messages like Beatles musician John Lennon's song "Imagine all the people, living life in peace." Even my mother cried at Mt. Luther King Jr.'s and John F. Kennedy's death – the death of hope. It was as if we were cut open in the middle of our lungs. More terrorist killings came, alongside the starry-eyed Lennon's assassination, leaving us bereft, along with his words, "Nothing to kill or die for . . .." Again, the extreme contrasts of love and hate in human nature made me endlessly determined to understand it all and ferociously question why. When a dilemma bugs you this much, you have to do something about it.

As Kennedy said in his Peace Speech, shortly before he was killed, *"We do not want a war . . . This generation of Americans has already had enough—more than enough—of war and hate and oppression . . . Confident and unafraid, we labor on—not toward a strategy of annihilation but toward a strategy of peace."* (Commencement address at American University, June 10, 1963, Washington D.C.)

The killing of Kennedy and others hit hard to our chests. The air was knocked out of us and society landed, kerplunk—down in the mud with more polarization, repression of women, and an upsurge of the whole big, dark muddy mess of human madness and brutality again. All of it was horribly harsh, a blast of contrasting disappointment again. I had become a counselor during all of it, helping people become whole and facilitating conflict in families. While seeing good people heal, I simultaneously felt helpless – viewing fractured politics and savage humans harming life. It made me agitated, itching the way you do when a spider sneaks up under your shirt, biting your back, leaving raw, red, bulbous marks hard to soothe in the night.

Metamorphosis requires sheltered spaces where we can hear ourselves and others, allowing us to penetrate inbred divides

Jump to 2023, now having been a psychotherapist for forty years, witnessing repair in my office, alongside my reading about constant war and violence everywhere. I scratched my scalp. The deep lines between my eyebrows permanently planted in my skull. How could people be resolving conflict in my office while the rest of the world was still destroying itself?

One reality during the day and another one hearing the news at night kept me half-awake in my sleep, flailing around, kicking my legs with karate chops. Mornings, I woke to pillows on the floor and bedding disheveled. The mirror showed me looking like Frankenstein's bride, eyes popping out of my head, frizzy hair standing straight on end.

So, here's the question: what makes positive change happen? Lasting transformation requires a deep dive. We all know we can create shifts that slowly creep back into the same old behaviors. But real remodeling comes from the ground up, the psyche and politics. Uprooting old ideas and emotions, replacing those with a new vision takes courage. People who have inspired positive paradigm shifts through history scoured their insides. Nelson Mandela, Mt. Luther King Junior, or great music like Leonard Cohen's *Hallelujah* arose from inner and outer wrestling – soul work.

When a dilemma bugs you this much, you have to do something about it.

It's vulnerable to "go down there." *Metamorphosis requires sheltered spaces where we can hear ourselves and others, allowing us to penetrate inbred divides.* Mandela had to go to jail and Cohen to a monastery. It doesn't need to be so severe, still, it's more urgent than ever now that we create local and far-reaching places for inner and outer dialogue. As Terry Patten writes, "An integral transformation of ourselves and our relationship to this larger web, and the discovery and development of new, holistic ways of being and doing are becoming evolutionary imperatives." He elaborates, "We are faced with being called to evolve beyond the exploitive, cannibalizing behaviors arising from narrow self-interest and to embody values that serve the greater good of the whole." (*A New Republic of the Heart*)

Unwittingly and unconsciously, we are in bed with war. Our loyalty to domination stems from deep imprinting. We believe that power above us is "a protective parent." As infants,

17

we needed someone to take care of us. A baby looks up to his parents to survive. We are habituated to authoritarianism. Underneath all our power struggles is the little kid who was told what to do so we robotically follow . . . like little chicks chasing their mother. *Our upbringing and the amygdala brain run us.*

With more education in the schools, learning about history, skilled communication, understanding anger, and valuing deep dialogue—*we can shift our present belief in the heroism of war and in the power of domination—to the power of dialogue. We can re-direct our fight or flight urges toward valuing our common good and collaboration. Our impulses to shut down, stonewall or attack can shift towards reparative conversations.*

I hope my experiences, vocation, and research lend proof to how change is possible. Some profound thinkers, as well, will bring credibility to a new way out of conflict, a quantum leap *from conflict to communion.*

So, here we go. But beware– along the way, I will become naked, showing you a few scars from my life. Our origins and stories always bring us to where we are.

INTRODUCTION

My interest in writing actually started while sending my diary entries to friends, spewing the days good and bad experiences. I called them emotional "hairballs." I got the idea from watching my cat. Einstein wagged his tail back and forth, in front of my computer screen as I frantically pecked away at the keyboard. Sometimes he'd release pent up, clogged stuff from his throat and look so serene afterward. I wondered, could humans get out their stuffed feelings, becoming calm like a cat? The hairball brings a bit of wit to an otherwise weighty topic: *How to Heal the People*. So, when you see that I've dropped a hairball into the writing, you'll know where it came from. As Naomi Klein jested, "a hefty dose of ridiculousness into the seriousness with which I once took my public persona." (*Doppelgänger*, NY Times, Oct. 1, 2023)

My friends weren't convinced that change could happen worldwide through the power of dialogue. They told me to give up the project. They said, "history repeats itself, you're not going to stop conflict." I get it. We're indoctrinated into the great glory of pounding our chests, the warrior. We've bought the belief that battle is bravery. We're so familiar with stories of strife or big money bulldozing, buying us out.

My community was cynical. "You can't stop global destruction." Colleagues shook their heads. I pleaded, "But, I believe in the evolution of the species." Discouragement has made it hard to keep my chin up. Their feedback made me feel like a hairy dog shaking itself off after a swim.

Still, I knew this paradigm shift was possible because I saw it every day. There had to be a parallel process. Our collective thrust toward complacency or anger is inbred and heavy, but I believe we can change direction. With just a few tools – reconnection replaces separation. Human beings can shift from being rude, awful, violent – pain in the asses – to communicative ones.

Resentment has to go somewhere.

It either gets turned inwards or out.

But, first, in order to re-direct anger we have to understand it. The little boy inside most savage shooters wasn't loved enough. He may not have been held or told he was talented. Maybe his parents ignored his cries, dominated him or never listened. The scenarios are infinite. But, in the end he (he/ she/they, LGBTQ+) spent his life withdrawn or enraged, locked up inside, wanting to be cherished or respected, seen and heard. Holding a gun to other beings was his strategy for getting noticed, an attempt at self-protection, belonging, an affiliation with some group or getting back.

The little kid deep inside eventually grows up to be some kind of character, maybe a hard working plumber with four kids or cheery, depressed, a workaholic, braggart, drinking too much, etc. Sometimes the child that was very polite in the sandbox, one day turns his head around, like an owl, pulling out dad's hunting ammunition and kills other kids. Maybe he's angry because they remind him of something. He envies them and projects his hatred onto them. Or perhaps he received harsh, humiliating words or whippings on his bare bottom, so he wants to retaliate somehow. Hurting other living beings is what we learn. *Resentment has to go somewhere. It either gets turned inwards or out.*

Our inner child still drives the bus. No wonder we numb out or dumb down. We seem blinded to our own destructive tendencies. Each time I circled this question: Why do humans continue to destroy and harm life? I felt stung by a hive of wasps. The topic of human cruelty was horribly painful. Maybe that's why there's not enough research on it.

Our species is embedded with prejudice and the glorification of attack.

Then I heard a hopeful story from a friend about a man who had pet rats. The way he loved them was touching. I thought of our contrasting inability to even design a way to redirect them to safer ground. All we do is kill life. It makes me sad. Rats are actually well meaning creatures, just trying to survive, like us. After all, we do share the world.

If only we could co-exist with each other and the land.

I needed to re-fuel somehow, do some self-care. So, I called a friend to take a walk on a sparkling spring day. We rambled along, chatting about all this – it was a sunny roadway, full of bright blooming daffodils in a serene neighborhood. Suddenly, a car screeched by us with two young boys in it. They rolled down their windows, shrieking and shouting. We jumped liked scared rabbits. My buddy muttered, "yeah, that is what we're talking about . . . " I slumped, asking, "what will it take for people to mature beyond rebellious kids with toy trucks and some kind of pistols?"

People are being gunned down in grocery stores and churches, through history in battlefields or during savage, brutal genocides. Our repetition compulsion continues . . ..

I had to find a way out. Understanding that the problem comes before the solution. The diagnosis is glaring: we all have splits in ourselves or between others. Our species is embedded with prejudice and the glorification of attack. It's everywhere: in the movies, the news, our neighborhoods, sports, our coffee clutches. *We are undereducated about how to hear each other*, instead we constantly witness one voice canceling out the other. The worst extension of rage is vicious, merciless killing of children and families on our earth, not to mention entitled thinking about being "above" races, groups, nature and animals. What is this rooted in?

Savagery and anger come from people full of fear and unmet needs. Centuries of wounding, from families being hurt for decades, from huge hatred for what "we" perceive as the enemy – this kind of fury runs through our veins. And, we all have some of it. Notice how you react to a car riding close to your back bumper, a sideways glance from a relative or a weird message on your phone. There are extreme examples and close to home, daily ones. The holocaust was one of many enormous slaughters of innocent families in recent history, not to mention the inhumane suffering of African American blacks and Indians in our background. Even animals are considered objects, "pigs," not intelligent. We're inundated with fighting and violence. Gabor Mate writes it well: "When trauma manifests on the political stage, the consequences for people and the planet are massive." (*The Myth of Normal*)

That round ball above our necks called the brain is a hazardous, complex machine. We all have different parts inside it, some of us manage them better than others. I can assure you though – the inner tyrant is in us all. You might paste on a smiley face, like a marionette, but just let someone cut in front of you in the grocery line or on the road. Your inner gangster will pop out.

Below awareness, unconscious to us – lies this judgmental voice. It takes many forms and shapes. We don't know why we get nasty, grumpy, sluggish, lethargic or blurry. This internal voice says: "Quit whining, you're too much" or "you're not enough . . . Why bother trying? You're a nag, too controlling, demanding. You're fat, flat or lazy. You'll never get it together." Listening to the voice of my inner critic makes me lay on the couch, eat chips and bread, stuffing my body with flour and water. It becomes a paste, like Elmer's glue, holding me down.

There are many sides to us all. We are each a bit like a kaleidoscope.

It's subtle at first, so I can hardly hear it, "Why don't you lighten up? You're a bottomless pit, a burden, too needy; your wishes are unrealistic, impossible . . . Get off the pity pot, you're too old, too big for your britches, etc." It sucks the life out of us, then we isolate, get moody, furious at others or curl up in a ball.

Before we know it, we aren't proactive. We don't even understand why. We are victims of our own psyche.

The good news is that: "No one is born hating another person because of the color of his skin, or his background, or his religion. People must learn to hate, and if they can learn to hate, they can be taught to love, for love comes more naturally to the human heart than its opposite." (Nelson Mandela, *Long Walk to Freedom,* 1994.) We can unlearn reflexive, ferocious slander and tyranny. We all carry false beliefs. Sometimes I ask clients, "What's the story you tell yourself?"

Our triggers live underground like lava waiting to explode.

There are many sides to us all. We are each a bit like a kaleidoscope. As Lawrence Durrell wrote, "to everyone we turn a different face of the prism." (*Justine / The Alexandria Quartet*)

Here's my wild hope: *Through my essays and true stories I want to ignite in you the courage to have crucial conversations – not argument.* It's not always easy, but urgent. **Valuing dialogue in all arenas is our way forward. Debate is just another war.**

By relaying to you what I see every day, the grief, vibrating renewal and wrestling matches inside and between my clients, they'll show us the way out of conflict. Their process demonstrates how we can hear each other, repair instead of ripping apart our communities and lives. At the moment humanity is failing, flailing around in fights and polarization.

My deepest wish is to move you off your chair, get you excited about your own power, re-direct despair, dispute and separation toward dialogue with dignity. My hope is that you will be moved to do: "radical reaching out." (A phrase given me by Sara Alexander, Psychotherapist.) Get involved in community endeavors, circulate in respectful conversations, hear each other, deeply, respectfully, patiently and insist on this value system in all governments and organizations.

Aren't we tired of all this insanity, school shootings, constant battles, extinct animals, the fear of hurricanes, floods and fires? We need a new narrative – a declaration of interdependence that ensures respect. More negotiations, not war. We even collude with large corporations owning us by not asking for fair practices! As trauma researcher Bessel Van der Kolk, M.D. summarized, *"The critical issue is reciprocity: being truly heard and seen by the people around us, feeling that we are held in someone else's mind and heart. For our physiology to calm down, heal, and grow we need a visceral feeling of safety. No doctor can write a prescription for friendship and love; these are complex and hard-earned capacities."* (The Body Keeps the Score)

Hate crimes have increased nearly 12% in 2021 over the previous year. (Federal Bureau of Investigation March 2023). "Half of all marriages end in divorce . . . second and third marriages fail at a far higher rate." (Forbes, *Revealing Divorce Statistics*, 2023 Bieber, J.D, Ramirez. J.D.) "65% of Americans are exhausted, 55% angry." (Pew Research, 2023)

Aside from constant conflict in our sphere, it's imperative that we understand rage has deep roots – most crime comes from people abused themselves, subtly or overtly. Referring to the rampage shootings in Uvalde to Allen, Texas, Dr. Petersen said, "in every case, literally . . . Perpetrators personal histories, directly influence their shootings." She reported, "The worse the crime, the worse the story." It's also known that many of these murderers leave prejudicial notes. (NY Times, 6/2022, Rachel Snyder)

Unless we investigate, we'll keep acting out feelings with fury. Swiss psychologist Alice Miller wrote: "All the childhood histories of serial killers and dictators I have examined showed them without exception to have been the victims of extreme cruelty . . . although they themselves steadfastly denied this. And in this they are not alone. Large sections of society are apparently determined either to deny or to ignore these facts." (*Drama of the Gifted Child*)

The things we've never said walk with us like a shadow, waking us up at night, when we most want to forget.

Our triggers (popular, weaponized term for emotional upsets) live underground like lava waiting to explode. Forgotten memories, old betrayals or past generations of trauma are still remembered *in our bodies*. Eventually our cover ups lose ground, gravel dribbles downhill, taking on momentum, then bombarding everything in sight. We're outraged or panicked by some minor thing and suddenly blast out in an eruption of some kind. You know the feeling? I found myself, just this week, blowing my stack in a group of women trying to enjoy an evening together. Out of the apparent "blue," I got pissed off at a stranger at the table because I heard a political opinion I didn't like. And I'm a psychotherapist, writing a book about diplomacy! I apologized but the damage was done. Trust is a fragile thing. The problem of unconscious rage is serious.

We fight, hide or implode. Or we're on "guard," or defend ourselves with the national guard, using *infant – try (infantry) to hurt, harm and destroy*. Our ability to deny and numb reality builds debris. Memories from years back remain tucked inside our psyche, contaminating our attitudes and behaviors, in the back of denied cupboards.

In Rwanda, the Tutsis and Hutus one day, after living side by side, became enemies. The ferocity and sadism of the murders is difficult to hear. In one province near the Tanzanian border, "over a thousand Tutsis were rounded up and taken to a church where the killers hacked at them with machetes all day. In the evening the killers immobilized those who were still alive by severing their Achilles tendons and went home to have a meal and sleep before returning to finish off the survivors." (*Raised to Rage*, Milburn and Conrad)

You can't have democracy without mental health.

They had lived side by side for years. Such separation and war come from something deep inside that is unexpressed. *The things we've never said walk with us like a shadow, waking us up at night, when we most want to forget.* Please don't turn away. We have to name our disease first before we can heal the people.

Richard Mollica, a Boston psychiatrist offers a stark explanation: "young males who have themselves been the victims of brutality – in the form of childhood abuse, social and political oppression, and past atrocities – and who are socialized to deny the true source of their anger and direct it outward against a scapegoat, are the most dangerous people on the planet." Whatever we deny, we repeat. Freud called it the "repetition compulsion." Face ourselves, we must.

A boiling pot like this globe needs a secure container. We used to rely on leadership, family or religion for stability, but those are fragmented now. At present, we diss-associate. "Many neighbors never talk in any meaningful way to their neighbors." And "60% of people in the U.S. right now report feeling lonely," (PBS.org 1/2023.) Even our daily lives include dislike of "the other" or conflict. It doesn't have to be that way. It will take all of us *leaning in.* It's just not enough to change laws or whittle regulations and rules around. Of course they matter. But, I believe if *we can't get along, we'll find a way to destroy whatever is in front of us.*

If my clients can unearth buried beliefs, and emotions and learn to speak respectfully, we all can. If they discover resolutions, putting their problems on the table, we can collectively change. It's stunning to watch their repair as they move away from conflict into communication. It's like seeing icy snowballs, tightly packed and frozen, on a winter day, ready for a fight, melting in the summer sun.

Our wounds are ancient. Even sweet cats are implanted with harmful instincts. Just this week I was delighted to see a bright, beaming blue bird in my back yard. On the next two mornings the local kitty killed both of her darling babies. My heart plummeted, seeing her lug them across the yard. They rarely even eat them. It's just their instinct, it's in their DNA.

I see couples and families argue about all kinds of things from affairs to what couch to buy. But, it's not about the couch. There are deeper psychic layers to be examined and "x-rayed." The *stories in our heads* can be projection, anxiety based, or sometimes true. Our beliefs wave like the wind, "you don't care about me because you're always late," or "I feel rejected because you never initiate contact," etc. Reconstruction arrives when we admit fears and remove armor, when we discover our distortions . . . maybe the other person wasn't thinking that at all?

Going down the ladder is one of the main tools. Together we discover our hidden selves, at each rung, staying curious, we find feelings or beliefs. Guilt, grief, confusion, shame, fear, inadequacy, resentment, longing or embarrassment reside inside. I sometimes call this work, playing "Sherlock Holmes." Together we discover and guess at unmet needs, unsaid wishes and generations of wounds still lingering inside us.

You can't have democracy without mental health. We need to be heard in safe communities and in political arenas. "The work" we do is like cleaning out old, dusty cupboards. When we wash all the dirt and grunge, syrupy molasses stuck to the boards, hairy strings of hidden grit from years back sicken us. We're a bit appalled but then relieved. Humanity has a lot of hurt tucked away. When we open ourselves to exploring our psyche through safe dialogue, we experience cleansing, lightness, and intimacy – *into me you see.*

But, we hide, even from ourselves – doing what I call the "Ostrich Thing." This year, the U.S. Surgeon General released a report titled ***Our Epidemic of Loneliness and Isolation:*** "In recent years, about one-in-two adults in America reported experiencing loneliness. And that was before the COVID-19 pandemic." He classified loneliness as a public health concern. (Vivek Murthy, May 3, 2023)

Richard Harwood wrote: **"When we do not go together as communities, we remain divided and fragmented. Loneliness becomes inevitable. Challenges mount and begin to look intractable** . . .We must go together. None of this means we all have to like one another. Nor can we sugarcoat our challenges. But going together requires, at a fundamental level, that we see and hear one another and make ourselves seen. I'm not saying we eliminate our differences. I'm not saying we pretend that division doesn't exist. Yet I am suggesting that we foster an ability to live with—*and lean into*—ambiguity, disagreement, and conflict *even as* we go together. We cannot afford to hunker down and continue retreating." (Sept. 19, 2023 The Christian Citizen, *We are Meant to go Together.*)

As you turn the page you'll move through my own memories of difficult dialogues. I hope my disclosures and personal stories demonstrate how repair happens. I decided to offer more of these rather than divulging too many private lives of all my clients.

BENCHES NOT FENCES

How DO we work through differences?

I got roused up writing this first chapter, so stirred by ideas like this one: if we all put benches in front of our homes, instead of fences, it could propel community conversations. I called dozens of furniture manufacturers asking for contributions to neighborhoods. This outer architecture alone might invite more joining and less dividedness.

Eric Klinenberg, in *Palaces for the People*, brought the idea home: "Social distance and segregation – in physical space as well as in lines of communication – breed polarization. Contact and conversation remind us of our common humanity particularly when they happen recurrently . . . . the hard work that lies before us will be impossible if we don't build better social infrastructure. The future of our democracy is at stake."

Let me put my head on the chopping block and let you in on a secret. Going through conflict is not easy for me either. And as I immersed myself in this topic, I kid you not, the wind

> *"Good fences make good neighbors."*
>
> – Robert Frost

blew the fence down between my neighbor's house and mine! "Seriously?" I thought, this is just too woo–woo. I called my editor, "I can't believe this is happening! How can I write about this while I'm in the middle of my own conflicted mess?" Okay, I know about synchronicity, but this was weird.

Anyway, all my poetic ideas about dropping walls and building bridges were lost in the shuffle of my pumping heart. "Who would pay for the repair? Should I eat the bill for the damned thing to keep the peace? Wasn't it her turn to step up? Last time there was a problem with our gate I took care of it myself!" Already a boisterous brawl was barking inside my head, blood pressure going up.

Perspiring through my blouse, I was wired for a fight. I know it sounds totally contrived, but really, my mind is a roller coaster when I'm nervous. I remembered Robert Frost's poem, *Mending Wall*, "Good fences make good neighbors . . . " My adrenalin skyrocketing, I was flooded with multiple thoughts simultaneously, not nearly as fun as multiple orgasms.

Here I was teaching people how to talk to each other in uncomfortable situations and I didn't want to do it! Thoughts racing, "Well, we had been friendly over the last year, hadn't we?" I wanted to bolt. Images of selling my house flew through

> *"Everyone has his own point of discouragement, his own wall. What you do when you hit this wall can spell the difference between helplessness and mastery, between failure and success."*
>
> – Martin Seligman

me. I hated my home in that split second, the hard work of owning it and now this!

It was like being in the front row of a film about a bloody boxing match. Stories crowded my head. Then I flashed on Frost again, he did not make fences sound friendly. "Something there is that doesn't love a wall . . . " His poem portrayed my frustration with barricades. Oh damn this stuff I was writing about. I did *not* want to talk about it with her!

I felt like a skunk, my back up, ready to spray. The image of walls is more upsetting to me these days, heightened with contentious, angry politicians building border walls, barricading families from each other, putting children in cages or separating them from their parents.

But I had to grab hold of myself. I remembered to ask, "what was my intention?" I tell people to figure out their aim going into a negotiation, but when you're under the gun yourself, theories flit by like hummingbirds, flapping wings at the speed of lighting, gone when you blink.

So, there I was, trying to do what I preach. I remind clients constantly, identify your true intention in a brawl. What was my wish? "Most of all," I kept telling her, "I want to keep our friendly feeling next door to each other." My body was tense, stomach tight, sphincter constricted. Sure enough, she mentioned insurance companies. She wanted to get a lot of estimates! Insurance people are a pain! All of that drags on into infinity.

Lock jaw syndrome returned. It tightens jaw muscles making it hard to open the mouth! I tried asking myself, "Okay, Katy, what do you want to do to create resolution?"

My busy brain darted around like a jumping bean, recalling this line from Martin Seligman's research on learned powerlessness: "Everyone has his own point of discouragement, his own wall. What you do when you hit this wall can spell the difference between helplessness and mastery, between failure and success." (*Learned Optimism*)

————

I admitted my

vulnerability

————

In my buzzing bee hive mind, I was quibbling with her. Then I realized, I was doing what I tell my clients not to! I really wanted to lurch at her with my resentments, like "YOU have to handle this. I did it last time!" But, insults and YOU statements could put the hair high on our backs. I saw a big cat fight coming . . . claws ready to slash out. Not such a good idea. So, "I" statements were my fall back plan, what I teach! I admitted my vulnerability and talked about how I had struggled with patching and fixing my big old house. I told her how anxious I was talking about all this. I made my own inner self known . . . *supportable*, seen and authentic.

Her head-butting softened. She opened up, saying she was worried about money too. I asked for my wishes, admitting I needed the lowest possible cost. There I stood – my stark naked self.

Fast moving emotions and thoughts are hard to manage when we're upset.

Damn, these unexpected conversations bring up every instinct all at once. "Should I be angrier and insist she pay for it?" I asked myself. But "shoulds" are often a sign of my own self-doubt. She started looking like a puffed-up bull again. I imagined her hoofing and scraping the ground. Now she wanted a more secure fence! I hopped backwards, *remembering to repeat my intention*, "I hope we can figure this out so it works for us both."

Luckily, she wanted something similar, which happens a lot if you get underneath "defensible space." *There's usually a treasure there.* We both said what we really wanted. We each craved ease and affordability. The up- shot? The fence was bolstered, repaired and supported by my handyman and so were we. It was a nail-biting conver- sation but we worked it out and we're still great neighbors. We didn't have to turn our backs on each other and hire insurance people or lawyers to stress us more. We expressed what we needed and found solutions. Bottled up emotions didn't have to suck our vibrant energy like a soured beer.

Being real opens the chest, the lungs; it's not guarded and tense. You enjoy life more.

You know, there are places that understand how to live together. In Zimbabwe, a team of grandmothers tackled depression in their community by sitting on benches, hearing what people needed to say. To date, the friendship bench exists in five different countries. The program has trained 700 health workers. (NIHR Global Mental Health Research, August 2022)

Our lives are threatened enough already, from the pandemic to hurricanes. We need each other more than ever, knowing that in a single instant, we could lose our electricity and heat or be taken over by tornadoes or earthquakes. "We use wealth to buy big houses with big yards that separate us and make us lonely." (David Brooks, *The Second Mountain*)

There is a wonderful relief and renewal that comes when we move *from Conflict to Communication*. Discovering remedies together is replenishing, jubilant, full of fun, infusing everyone with new hope. Gloria just brought me fruit from her tree today! It's like getting your golf ball out of a sand pit.

As Robert Provine wrote in his scientific investigations on laughter itself: "Solitary chimps, like solitary people, seldom laugh, a result consistent with laughter's role as a social signal. But chimps and humans differ in the social situations in which they laugh – we humans have added something new to our still present chimp like tendencies. Adult humans laugh most during conversation." (Laughter*: A Scientific Investigation*)

Being triggered is tricky. Our lizard brain takes over, making it incredibly challenging to stay centered in the storm. I needed to take a lot of deep breaths and short breaks away from talking to my neighbor. A pause can help us, a sort of cease fire. Susan Campbell describes possibilities in her book, *From Triggered to Tranquil*: "You pause in order to give everyone time to get calm and reassure themselves that they are not in any real danger." The important thing is to be authentic and respectful, returning to the conversation to find resolution.

But, we stay close to the chest instead, tethered to technology. Left to our own devices (excuse the pun) we retreat to technology. Avoidance works for awhile and eventually, not so much.

Being real opens the chest; it's not guarded and tense. You enjoy life more, without a tight neck. As Catherine Price researched there are three elements to having fun: playfulness, connection and flow. (*The Power of Fun.*) Connection arrives from communication.

FEAR and FAÇADE

What gets in the way of working through Conflict?

Robert Putnam put his finger on the peoples' pulse: "We are less likely to turn out for collective deliberation – whether in the voting booth or the meeting hall – and when we do, we find that discouragingly few of our friends and neighbors have shown up." (*Bowling Alone.*) When we do, "We maintain a façade of formal affiliation, but we rarely show up. We have invented new ways of expressing our demands that demand less of us."

Why are we so stuck in isolation, cynicism and violence? FEAR. It fuels our combativeness or avoidance behaviors. But, we deny it. Fear is a *taboo* subject consistently in my work. So, it remains unconscious. In sessions with families, when I guess that fear exists, I hear the inevitable, "well, maybe concern, not fear." Then I pry, "what about "worry?" The reflex is consistent, "oh maybe

Fear is the most primitive emotion on the planet. It makes us quarrelsome or complacent. But, we don't talk about it; we compartmentalize it . . . tuck it away with embarrassment.

worry . . . but not fear." Why? There's no doubt it's running through our world and our bodies. The topic of anxiety bugged me throughout this writing, like a mosquito buzzing in my ear at midnight in the heat of summer. "What, me worry?" I guess Mad magazine had it right, if you are old enough to remember Alfred E. Neuman.

Fear is the most primitive emotion on the planet. It makes us quarrelsome or complacent. But, we don't talk about it; we compartmentalize it . . . tuck it away with embarrassment.

Men especially recoil in counseling when I guess that they might be "afraid." No, no, no, it's never fear . . . maybe "suspicion or concern." *Admitting fear is taboo. But, I find it turns the dial in family therapy, wakes up important connection, when it is named.* Admitting "I am afraid" is a part of being real, I call it: "audacious authenticity." Once it's admitted, you can actually see people lean toward each other. "Oh, I didn't know my tone scares you."

We're all mixed up about what power is. We're ashamed of true emotions like fear. Brene Brown characterizes courage as this: "share all of yourself." She mentions the anxiety coursing through us especially since 9/11. (Ted Talks, 12/23/2010 The *Power of Vulnerability*.) I believe there is also terror in our bodies, since the horror of the holocaust. We are afraid. Martha Nussbaum writes, "Fear lies at the heart of primary disgust . . . " in *The Monarchy of Fear*. Sometimes we're even repulsed by a simple foreign odor in another individual, We've absorbed, like sponges, the wrong idea about what power is. Judging others is not justice, it's not what we're born to do – it builds anxiety everywhere.

I hesitate to bring this up, but even sports encourage our adoration of strength. Yelling or screaming together about a victory! Sure, there's some fun in it. I enjoy a tight butt or a tight game sometimes. But, when we identify with one side we can even erupt in fights. I see people more upset over their team losing a game than the starving children in Africa. Ezra Klein writes about how our identity politics can be a problem: "Sports are such a powerful force in human society precisely because they harness primal instincts that pulse through our psyche." In other words, he writes: "What we are often fighting over in American politics is group identity and status. . . . Those merged identities attain a weight that is breaking our institutions and tearing at the bonds that hold this country together." (*Why We're Polarized*)

Fear is important.

It can quiet us or make

us mad. It's best when we

attend to it – it points us

to our yearnings.

Right now we express anxiety or needs like kids throwing their food on the floor. So, instead of clear thinking or authentic emotions, we have cognitive "distance." We shove real emotions down or project anger onto others. We use our egos to attack "the other." Brene Brown describes our present struggle about weakness and pride: "Feelings are for losers and weaklings." She adds, "I think of my ego as my inner hustler. It's always telling me to compare, prove, please, perfect, outperform, and compete." (*Rising Strong: The Reckoning. The Rumble. The Revolution.*) The ego owns us. But, "vulnerability is the birthplace of everything we crave" . . . It opens gates. (*Super Soul*

Sunday / 3/17/2013/ Brene Brown / Oprah interview.) *In fact, we are getting heart attacks, bad backs, auto immune diseases and other symptoms while absorbing the tension of our frightening environment. Emotional pain has no place to be processed.*

Fear is important. It can quiet us or make us mad. It's best when we attend to it – it points us to our yearnings. It craves respect and coming out of the closet. As Thomas Jefferson said, "All tyranny needs to gain a foothold is for people of good conscience to remain silent." Our dissociation from feeling has allowed us to turn our heads from atrocities. The ego wants its way with us. It protects our soft center. "No problem in judgement and decision-making is more potentially catastrophic than overconfidence," insists Wesleyan social psychologist Scott Plous. "Its consequences include the Chernobyl disaster, the sinking of the Titanic, the Challenger and Columbia space shuttle disasters, and the Deep Water Horizon oil spill, among many others."

Once, I had a teacher who said, "I know when I'm telling the truth because I feel embarrassed."

Psychologist Daryle Van Tongeren said, "Curious collaborative inquiry has been abandoned for the brute force of unilateral persuasion," writes Bruce Grierson. "Call it cognitive narcissism." (*The Certainty Trap*, Psychology Today, July 2023)

Fear can guide us to our deepest needs. It would mean a new narrative to us if we could admit "I am afraid," without shame. We all have different parts. But, blaring, brutish anger is still considered more heroic. We value blasting the birds for fun on hunting weekends above caring for wildlife. Fear is a culprit that can weaken us or be a blessing. I watch couples at their pivotal moment, when they move out of their intractable arguments. It's often when the most embarrassing truth unfolds: "I'm afraid that you don't find me attractive" or "I'm afraid you don't want to spend time with me." Fear is a sweet spot, a melting pot. It invites intimacy. Nobody wants to say, "I'm afraid you don't love me," but it *brings down walls*.

I still blush when I tell anyone I'm afraid. I wait for their kick ass advice to "get over it," just "pull up your big girl panties," etc. It takes courage to identify our fears in a culture that *does not acknowledge they exist*. It requires us to stand up for the chink in our armor. It's like pushing big boulders aside to train your friends to respect emotions. I tell them sometimes, "advice is not what I need, just hear me." They learn – if you ask.

Fear is a sweet spot, a melting pot. It invites intimacy.

Once, I had a teacher who said, "I know when I'm telling the truth because I feel embarrassed." (Cherie Carter Scott.) Since then, the rising hot pink in my cheeks is my measure of honesty. Susan David, Harvard Medical School Psychologist refers to the "tyranny of positivity" in which you should never cry at work but "if you can't help it then for goodness sake do it quietly in a bathroom stall." She mentions "wearing a public smile and vomiting up ice cream in private." The more you ignore feelings, the bigger they get like the chocolate cake you know is in the refrigerator. (Susan Cain, *Bittersweet: How Sorrow and Longing Make Us Whole*)

What's the result of our collective coercion to be

successful, dishonest or always smiling, the "happy face?" People bursting at the seams with road rage, shooting innocents, broken relationships, job turnover, cars spinning out of control or demolishing the "other." ***Buried emotions have to go somewhere.***

Sometimes I even wonder about the secrecy of psychotherapy. Why do we live in a world that avails us a single place in society to open? It's usually a white office, with a plant half sagging in the corner and a corridor to wait in, while reading Glamour or Travel magazines. Or, we're behind computer screens, talking to a stranger about our feelings at a high cost for fifty minutes? We're squeezing a lifetime of stories into that?

I don't want to eject myself out of business. I believe my profession is pivotal in the rearranging of a society prevalent with prejudice, separation and bloodshed. I just wish humanity had more access to shameless sharing. I'd like to see Relationship 101 taught in schools, with communication skills, civil rights, morality and critical thinking starting from kindergarten on up. *What if we learned about the roots of anger – to understand and redirect it?* I'd like to see clients learning not to depend on therapy but to build the courage to communicate respectfully in their relationships. With tech talk becoming our future, between doctors' lawyers or families – it will be more important than ever that we learn to connect and communicate.

> *"Tyranny of positivity"*
>
> *in which you should*
>
> *never cry at work but "if*
>
> *you can't help it then for*
>
> *goodness sake do it quietly*
>
> *in a bathroom stall."*
>
> – Susan David

I'd like to see more places for meaningful conversation. Klinenberg's idea in *Palaces for The People,* is relevant: "In a world where we spend ever more of our time staring at screens, blocking out even our most proximate human contacts, public places with open door policies compel us to pay close attention to people nearby." A "lack of connection can increase the risk for premature death to levels comparable to smoking 15 cigarettes a day." (U.S. Surgeon General, May 2023.) Robert Puttnam, in *Bowling Alone,* describes brilliantly how important "social capital" is. "People divorced from community, occupation, and association are first and foremost among the supporters of extremism."

I am uplifted, walking into our local Irish pub in Sonoma. When I wander through, I hear cheer from friends and glorious music. My stress level shifts. Within minutes I'm surrounded by humor and chat. Whether book clubs, town parks or bocce ball, we need each other. "An increase in the number of neighborhood coffee shops is associated with a decrease in the number of murders." (Chicago Police Dept., U.S Census / *Palaces for the People* / Eric Klineneberg)

Openness needs to be valued, inclusive architecture created. No more top-down designs. All endeavors could be re-configured – theater could engage the audience in a round arena, all on one level, political debates don't need more stages, with figures up above us, but on the same floor with us and affordable housing meetings designed for togetherness – with no more "higher ups."

Bring down the podium and proscenium, nobody stands above. Let the people speak.

THE PINK SWEATER

When We Don't Speak Up –
The Losses and Consequences

It's an honor to be invited into my client's private terrain. It's like dipping under the sea while snorkeling, visiting an infinitely inspiring, mysterious, underworld, filling me with awe. Sometimes there's damage, like fish caught in snarly nets, scary darkness or we peer at pulsing, enlivening, revelatory life.

I have buried shipwrecks of my own. My past, along with the courage my clients loan me, propel this writing. So, I invite you to enter, even though looking into our personal history can be like using a rusty screwdriver to pry open a corroded, nailed tight door. But, "going down there" is necessary, because as Freud said, "the patient does not remember anything of what he has forgotten and repressed, but acts it out." ***We repeat old patterns unless we shine a light on them.*** (1914 *Remembering and Working Through*)

So, with you as my witness, we'll do a deep dive:

There was almost nothing so exciting as being with my brawny, broad shouldered brother. I adored him. Every time we got together it was thrilling. I wanted to tell everyone,

'Hey, here's my big brother.' Standing beside him, it was as if nothing could ever hurt me again.

We had a blast being together, jogging, sweating through our shirts playing racquetball, grabbing a drink and flirting with people at the bar. We bubbled over like shaken champagne, just being together. I flew from San Francisco. He came from San Diego to Seattle to visit Mom. I couldn't wait to see him with that wild smile beaming back at me. Like jumping puppies, we skipped through the airport, chattering, hurling our bodies toward each other with huge hugs.

We always expected a good time, forgetting about mom's sudden rage attacks. We compartmentalized well, like little tail wagging pups still weaning and wanting their mother. It could happen anytime, anywhere – at Thanksgiving, a birthday party or an expensive restaurant, but we always pretended it didn't happen.

Her fiery vengeance was piercing and usually pointed at him, like hurling hot, burning coals. But, Lee kept hoping for her love. He became like the chubby kid he once was, playing the clown, telling her jokes. I was the special one, carefully tucked into my polite, pleasing mode. *I had discovered my own best defense. He had his.*

We used to let her rant and criticize, then we'd shut down. Our habit, well learned from dad, who listened to her outrage nightly, while he closed up like a snail with salt poured on it.

Sometime after we dropped our baggage at moms, Lee ran across the street for

It's strange how you can be an adult and still act like a child around your parents.

a quick trip to the shopping mall. Later, he leaped back into the living room. To me he seemed like Superman. Springing to his shopping bag, he held up his newly purchased pink pastel sweater. Soft colors were popular for men that year.

I thought it complimented him. I was infatuated by the softness of it, next to his bold, robust muscles. This was my big brother – a man's man. He loved to watch sports and hang out with friends. Women puffed up like peacocks around him, wallowing in his rare wit and warmth. Kindness oozed from him, alongside his manly strength. Sometimes friends would ask me if he was a priest.

"When dialogue dies, as it can with either person's failure to speak, to hear, or to acknowledge the other, then part of the self also dies."

– Dana Jack

All I remember after he held up that sweater was Mom's pulsing, red neck, her mouth suddenly spitting venom – vicious, cruel words. She went ballistic. It must have been some kind of trigger. Her fury was like ammunition gunning him down.

I don't recall exactly what she said, just the way the air felt, as if full of blood after a killing. He didn't say anything more. He went straight to bed, even though it was the middle of the day. All I remember was stony silence in the house, except the sound of clinking ice cubes as she poured her late afternoon vermouth Manhattan.

It's strange how you can be an adult and still act like a child around your parents. After the onslaught, I have no idea what happened. We probably ate a lot of cookies and acted nice the next day. *There is such a strong grip on us sometimes, a gravitational pull to shut down.* Five months later Lee had a major stroke. He never walked or talked again.

He spent the last fifteen years of his life in a nursing home, in diapers, laying there. He had absorbed Mom's loathing, like a sponge.

If I had admitted my fears, asked for what I wanted, it might have bolstered both Lee and me. I could have told her how frightening she was. I could have asked for what I needed. I don't know if she would have changed, but I imagine somewhere inside her, she would have heard me and so would Lee. And I know I always stand taller – when I have my voice. As Dana Jack wrote in *Silencing the Self,* *"When dialogue dies, as it can with either person's failure to speak, to hear, or to acknowledge the other, then part of the self also dies."*

If only I'd said, "I don't want to listen to you rage anymore. Mom, it's a sweater."

If I had said something, there's a chance he might still be my big brother.

IN THE BEGINNING
was the Wound . . .
and the way out

Humanity's ability to cover up our true selves is astounding. We say we're "fine, fine, fine" when we've got gout or panic attacks. Strong silent types might be secretly depressed or we could suffer addictions and maladies, related to forgotten memory. There is a split inside each of us, with disassociated parts.

Even the big U.S. defends its ego. We spend trillions to keep battles going, only to end up negotiating in the end. While heat waves ravage children and elders, rapes threaten and terrify young girls all over the world, elephant's tusks are slashed and sold, we're just "fine."

Getting underneath our shields and patterns takes detective work and courage. It's essential to learn about ourselves and how to re-direct our destruction of the planet – like crawling into the ignored attic to see what's there. What's this anger really about? It requires guessing and discipline – learning to regulate our reactions and understand them is worthy work. As Erich Fromm wrote in *The Art of Loving*, "Love is active concern." He likens it to learning the guitar or any important endeavor.: "Is LOVE an art? Then it requires knowledge and effort. Or is love a pleasant sensation, which to experience is a matter of chance, something one 'falls into' if one is lucky?" Like any important endeavor, "it always implies certain basic elements. . . . These are care, responsibility, respect and knowledge."

What triggered my mom about the color of a sweater? There must have been many stories lurking in her unconscious. Maybe the color pink reminded her of her own brother, cut out of their mother's inheritance because he was gay in a decade that made it terribly taboo. He suffered many years from that abandonment. I will never know the whole truth because I didn't brave that conversation with her.

Do you yell at the weeds for growing back each spring, even through thick cement?

We desperately need to witness each other's wounds, tell our stories without being questioned, advised or shamed. Your archives, the generations before you – are implanted in you. I saw my mother repeat what she learned. She was scolded and abused by a barbaric father. She only talked about it once, when I forced the conversation. "Mom, why do you have so much rage all the time?" She seemed to shrink in front of me, looking like a small child, telling me how her dad yelled at her, scolding her, telling her she was repulsive, an ugly child. Tears stormed her eyes. Then, she roughly brushed them aside with her hands, like an annoying, leaky spigot. She sneered – the Jekyll Hyde I knew so well. She scoffed, then there was no more crying, just a weird cackling sound. Mom moved her eyes sideways, seeming to watch a faraway memory. Grunting, she told me she laughed when her dad died, that it was the best day of her life. He was shot in a barroom brawl.

Both of our lives might have been changed if I had heard more of her stories. *We don't lose power, we gain it – by revealing our aches and sorrows. We all need reverent witnesses for our struggles.*

Our wounds wind around us like unexpected cyclones, swooping up our lives. If we don't discover them and decide on a new way to live, they run us. The repetition compulsion is well in place – we act out the same habits over and over that we've adopted. I see it happen in my therapy office often, as my eyes bug out of my head. It's like sitting in the front row facing a massive movie screen, watching harrowing, family fights or sudden silence, while being hit with a stun gun.

In my office, someone rolls their eyes at a family member, "I thought we talked about this before. Do we have to go over it again?" I often use analogies to help people understand their own underworld; I say, "*Do you yell at the weeds for growing back each spring, even through thick cement? God damn it, stop growing in my yard? You expect them and know that eventually, you have to dig down, to their roots.*"

I believe our planet can only be healed through more insightful inquiry, education, teaching the kids and adults communication skills, do-able conflict resolution tools, learning to comprehend and regulate our anger and available counseling.

I sometimes imagine couples with a huge water balloon that they are holding up between them as they argue. When it breaks, the baby is born.

Our personal problems are replicated in politics. We can debate, chastise or throw spit wads, change laws, policies, build better freeways, jobs, affordable housing, more trained police, volunteer to help – all activism matters. But, in the end, we have to learn to bridge divides, inside and around us. *The personal is political.*

I, frankly, don't know that we necessarily need multiple college degrees and licenses to be competent counselors. Sure, the training I've received contributed to my mastery. But – good listening and caring goes a long way.

It's curative to be heard in a safe place. When Allen Ginsberg (*one of the world's best poets*) told his psychiatrist he wanted to be a poet, he responded, "why not?" Can you imagine if he'd been told to become a dentist? Safe, being the key word here. Who wants to tell the truth when you're *afraid* of getting lectured, fired, losing friends and colleagues, divorce, etc.?

> *"The critical issue is reciprocity: being truly heard and seen by the people around us, feeling that we are held in someone else's mind and heart."*
>
> – Bessel Van Der Kolk

We have to get underneath façades. They are dangerous. You've heard in the news enough about how the neighbor who always seemed so sweet and generous ended up murdering his entire family, etc.

There's a certain dead wood that petrifies our bodies and the earth's when we're afraid to speak up. We leave that to the whistle-blowers, but it's also up to us.

WHAT'S AT THE BOTTOM OF ALL THIS ANGER?

The Inner Critic

Our human propensity to hate stems from the tyrant inside us all.

It shows up often in males, as agitation, impatience or pointed outward, as anger. In females the inner critic can be directed inward – telling us we're inadequate – causing self-doubt or criticism of ourselves or others. It is often louder in females because we did not inherit a belief in our entitlement, making us instead, compliant or coy. In any gender, the inner critic is a problem.

"Through voice, we locate ourselves in the world and can be heard and found."

– Dana Jack

The bully inside is hard to catch, saying: "Not for you; maybe for other people, but not for you." This critic causes ceaseless worry and undercuts dreams. Mary Beard captured women's long history, "When it comes to silencing women, Western culture has had thousands of years of practice. And most of the rest of the globe has not empowered us either."

I can tell you, it makes my pulse race to hear clients talk of their inner terrorist. It's shocking. They literally turn white in the room. I can see the cutting off of their life force, their faces look like horrified Dracula victims.

This force has to be recognized. Otherwise, we will continue to point our fingers outward at everyone else. When we dislike or belittle ourselves, we are easily threatened or revengeful of others. The inner terrorist can make us puff up like immense monsters or weigh us down, like a heavy anchor lunged far into dark waters, tugging us to the bottom of the sea, where we're smothered.

In men, it often shows up as shutting down, for fear of feelings. For females, it wasn't that long ago that we did not have the right to vote. We've been dragged through the streets and be-headed during witch hunts, hung or scalded for not covering our faces, cooking dinner or for flirting. We are imprinted with centuries of belittling.

We are rumbling and boiling, like lava under the earth waiting to erupt for centuries. Not willing to be dismissed, scorned, burned, talked down to, raped, seen as objects or inadequate any longer, time's up.

We want our voices. As Dana Jack writes, "Through voice, we locate ourselves in the world and can be heard and found." (*Silencing the Self.*) My mother fought for her words, in a time when women wore petite Easter hats and crossed their legs. The desire to express our full selves is ancient in us. Phoebe Waller-Bridge wrote: "Being proper and sweet and nice and pleasing is a fucking nightmare. It's exhausting" she exclaims, "As women, we get the message . . . to be a good, pretty girl from such an early age. Then at the same time, we're told that well-behaved girls won't change the world or ever make a splash. Well, what the fuck am I supposed to be? . . . a really polite revolutionary?" Phoebe spreads her arms and starts to laugh, "It's impossible." *(Women and Hollywood, 7/2017)*

The inner terrorist weighs us down or makes us crabby. Its force is daunting. I remember the day I decided to start jogging. That moment is unforgettable. I fought with my critic as it sat on me, sapping my energy. I forced myself to put on my black running bra, and pulled on those God-awful tight stretchy black tights that

"You're making a mountain out of a molehill; how dare you; you've brought it up so many times before, get over it."

people jog in. I walked as if a brick was tied to each shoe, telling myself this was a stupid idea. As I moved, my feet lifted, one, then the other. I soared down the street, breaking through its tyranny, even though it tried to tie me up with barbed-wire, telling me I wasn't in the mood. I broke away from the critic's clutches.

It was an unforgettable moment because the literal sensation of heaviness dispersed. I wasn't really tired, the negative voices were making me sluggish, as if walking in sticky molasses (abuse is exhausting.) I was almost convinced not to try. This is serious stuff in all genders, but women have an extra dose from centuries of being subjugated or abandoned. As Clarissa Pinkola Estes wrote, "Mother of God! So many women themselves are afraid of women's power. If men are going to ever learn to stand it, then without a doubt women have to learn to stand it." (*Women Who Run with The Wolves*)

How to harness the internal monster? It's similar to external tyrants. First, we have to note the signs when it is happening. For some it might be the slow taking over of our towns by wealth, or crimes infiltrating our communities. For me, it's often a sense of defeat, lethargy or wanting to devour flour. That's when I have to tell myself something supportive. The other day my inner critic was berating me. It was like a beating, creating an echo chamber in my head. I finally yelled out loud to it, "get off my back!" Sometimes I have to call a friend or text Sylvia, "time for a hairball?" Just getting it out and hearing it helps me. On other days, taking a walk, or telling it to go away, it will slowly unleash its ball and chain.

> "*When people experience life in a domination system, they tend not to see that there exist more equitable and compassionate, and less stressful and damaging, life options.*"
>
> – Riane Eisler

There will probably always be a part of me that wants to drag me down. I can stop my self-doubt and shaming more often now though – because I recognize it. When I am reluctant to move, to risk, to speak up, sinking into powerlessness, when a fog sweeps over me, it's the critic's claws in me . . . it's time for a rest or re-fuel.

We, the people, can only be stomped on when we allow

ourselves to be victims, "Remember, this power of the people on top depends on the obedience of the people below: workers go on strike, huge corporations lose their power." (Howard Zinn with Amy Goodman.) We can rise above our helplessness. The tyrant inside is not in complete power over most of us.

At my writing group this week the most gifted woman in the room read her writing to us and called it "boring." She was incredibly talented, but could hardly hear us when we told her how brilliant she was.

Abusive, often subtle voices we don't quite identify reside inside: "You're making a mountain out of a molehill; how dare you; you've brought it up so many times before, get over it." Disapproval waits for us in hidden corners of our being.

The inner critic is a gargantuan source of destruction and death. It causes politicians and leaders to do harm and others to follow them. It can be inherited for generations – an insidious sub-personality. Then we do awful, unthinkable acts. In Rwanda, how do you suppose that within only one hundred days so many human beings could "Kill those Tutsi; we let them go last time;" kill their children; murder friends, saying "don't let the cockroaches survive." How could anyone step right up to a pregnant woman, children and families, slaughtering them? We might call this incomprehensible, but it is also resides in all of us – this capacity to terrorize. Death by demonization pervades the planet. Are we listening to our demons? This destructive instinct lives in most of us in different degrees from being uncaring to shunning, being passive aggressive or more harmful acts.

We learn there is nothing wrong with the use of force

if we grow up with bullying or idealize it. Studies continue on why obedience to authority is so frequent, causing unconscious cruelty. Stanley Milgram and others have researched this inbred instinct. (PsyPost.org, 2/1/2024, Dolan) Riane Eisler and Douglas Fry capture this in their studies of "power over" politics . . . "when people experience life in a domination system, they tend not to see that there exist more equitable and compassionate, and less stressful and damaging, life options." (*Nurturing our Humanity*)

Unfortunately, many of our actions are often taken with a lack of responsibility. But all have consequences, which for many, are harmful, even deadly. What we need to encourage is critical thinking or more morality. Do to others, as you would have them do to you. And mean it.

But there is hope for future generations. I see young people enter my office, full of potential and creativity, with vibrating, throbbing life force and fervor, only to admit their inner judges exhaust them, causing depression or other problems. It's depleting to doubt oneself and our abilities. Unable to protect themselves from the onslaught of a pressurized, competitive culture, they still make it to my office. Some part of them has persistence, knows there is a better way to live. Some part inside them knows a life with love in it would be better, that they are okay, maybe even much more than okay – maybe great.

They seek me out because a small voice inside them says, "Let's get support." They learn to redirect old beliefs and behaviors, shifting self-hate and anger to empathy and patience with others and themselves.

TELLING THE TRUTH
AND TRANSFORMATION

Good listening and caring goes a long way. Carl Rogers, one of the fathers of psychology said: "*When someone really hears you without a passing judgement on you, without taking responsibility for you, without trying to mold you, it feels damn good . . . When I have been listened to and when I have been heard, I am able to perceive my world in a new way and to go on. It is astonishing how elements which seem insoluble become soluble when someone listens.*"

Words unsaid keep us disempowered. When we're terrified of telling the truth, we point out the faults in others.

I'm just saying . . . we need *more* education about civility, teaching the kids do-able communication skills and affordable counseling. I'm not saying all counselors are adequate, but we need more trained facilitators, setting the tone for non-judgmental conversation.

We crave connection, but without safety, we pull back. And, when we stop circulating we're dead. Still, who wants to tell the truth when you're afraid of getting fired, losing friends and colleagues, divorce, etc.? So, we're life-less, afraid or furious instead. Asserting our needs is threatening. Without a supportive social environment, we succumb to the temptation to look the other way.

Soldiers, even those who have been regarded as heroes, complain bitterly that no one wants to know the real truth about war. "When the victim is already devalued (a woman, a child), she may find that the most traumatic events of her life take place outside the realm of socially validated reality. Her experiences become unspeakable." (Judith Herman, M. D.)

Our sorrow blows us apart when we admit how hurt we have been. "The descent into mourning is at once the most necessary and the most dreaded task of this stage of recovery. Patients often fear that the task is insurmountable, that once they allow themselves to start grieving, they will never stop." (*Trauma and Recovery*, Herman)

Whether we get IBS or migraines, bad backs, gout, strokes, kidney disease, auto-immune diseases, cancer or other ailments – a fragmented society contributes to disease. Even our doctors or organizations don't talk to each other, one practitioner to another. Not to mention, they have no time to talk to us.

"Why, over the two decades, have we seen this epidemic of loneliness and meanness?

. . .

It's about teaching the basic social and emotional skills so you can be kind and considerate to the people around you."

– David Brooks

How can that create cohesion in our bodies or the body of our earth? There is no communication inside ourselves and between each other.

Words unsaid between us, shunning and withholds – keep us disempowered. When we're terrified of telling the truth, we point out the faults in others.

We even project our disowned "inferior" traits onto others, then we condemn, desecrate or even exterminate them. As long as we don't have to admit our imperfect selves, we can believe we are adequate. We can place our own self disdain on others. The importance of being superior is built into us. We even dismiss nature and animals as objects or resources. This way we can absolve ourselves of any weak parts that might not be above it all.

When I worked as a supervisor in a mental health agency, I created collaborations called "systems of care." We were stunned at the increased power we had when we joined and heard each other's struggles and triumphs, when we worked in teams instead of alone, helping families with mental health needs. Lawyers, County Managers, Probation, Foster Care, In Home Case Workers, Administrators, etc. *When we sat at the table we became like a locomotive. Suddenly we were moving in the same direction.* We were a trillion times more dynamic, knowing each other, having personal contact. I wish I had words to capture how those table talks thrust us forward. The work was hard and angst producing. When

We have a huge responsibility to change our history of cruelty.

We can do it.

inevitable tension heightened, the usual issues, like "not returning phone calls," "no shows," etc. *Repeating the intention* quelled our grudges, returning us to our coalitions. We need collaboration to sustain helpful services. I had to repeat our *intention* at each meeting many times, "we are here to help the families." Intention has great power. A small framed fifteen year old ran to his father laying under a truck lifting the huge vehicle off of him, saving his life. These and many such stories prove the point, repeatedly. (12/5/2022, ABC/7)

One memory seems important to tell. I finally met the head of Mental Health. We sat with colleagues, troubleshooting, trying to find ways to assist a young boy with parents on heroine, lost in the system. These were all the top notch professionals in our field. The Director bowed, putting his hand to his shaking head. When he looked up, a crease burrowing between his eyes, he muttered, "you mean to tell me none of us sitting here can figure out how to help this kid?" Our grief in the room that day was thick. Sharing our impotence was as important as ambition. Instead of resentfully checking boxes and collecting pay checks, we cared – together – in our hearts and groins – all the way from the top – down. We need all systems to come to the table, often – police, prison executives, foster care workers, budget administrators, politicians, authentically.

One thing could change everything . . . valuing conversation everywhere. True dialogue does not want one person above another. As Daniel Yankelovich writes in *The Magic of Dialogue,* "higher-ranking people have, for the occasion, removed their badges of authority and are participating as true equals." *Families or couples constantly tell me that what helps them more than anything is committing to a weekly time to have dialogue. It sounds so simple, but it is the glue.*

Becoming skilled at "holding" places with conflict will be more and more urgent going forward. "This generation of Americans has a rendezvous with destiny." (Thom Hartmann, *The Crash of 2016: The Plot to Destroy America.*) We have a huge responsibility to change our history of cruelty. We can do it.

If you think of ants, they get in a line, go up a hill and bring bread crumbs to the top. They accomplish it as a team. According to Deborah Gordon, biology Professor at Stanford, "Ants are not smart . . . but colonies are smart." Ants accomplish amazing things, they don't just leave their "fellow ants" alone when carrying huge objects, they help each other, making it possible to achieve their goals. They communicate consistently, it's by scent, and it works.

There are individuals who make a difference too. Whistleblowers, authors, artists, leaders, everyday people too. I don't want to diminish the idea that some people are great, moral leaders, *but I want us all to become them – to own our inner heroes.* We need each other. Why not call for The Constitution of Inter-Dependence?

FRIENDSHIPS, RELATIONSHIPS, MENDING THE DIVIDE

So often we pretend everything is OK and just pull away. Friendships too can be a challenge. Cassandra was a former roommate of six years. We enjoyed tons of good times together, fixing up the house and chatting. But our ongoing arguments ended in stony silence. In spite of our attempts to talk, it seemed to take more balls than I had. So, she moved out.

One day, years later, I heard a loud, pounding knock on the front door. Opening it, there she stood. We were both bone tired, from the unbelievable California 2017 fires that swept our region, watching flames all around, destroying homes in seconds, like kindling. I waved Cassandra to come in.

It was the first big fire in Sonoma County. I had tried to get some sleep, coughing from being in the suffocating air and a smoke filled house, with little luck. She was barely dressed, terrified, dislocated, wearing a torn shirt she threw on while racing to escape flames and blocked roads at her home high up on the hill. She stood there with her three dogs and a huge, wire cat carrier.

In shock, I must have looked as if someone plugged me into an electric socket, my dry, kinky hair sparking toward the ceiling. I stared at Cassandra with her long curls pulled back in a bun, looking destitute. The smell of smoldering embers smothered my old wooden house. Smoke seeped into curtains and lodged into the floor boards. A menacing odor, like black char burning after leaving food too long on the stove penetrated everything. Ashes covered our cars and laid thick on our furniture, loading our lungs.

It's hard to explain the force of fire. It's savage, primitive, uncontrollable power ripping through trees and roofs. I could see it in the distance, over the rooftops, miles away, flying forward and back, flipping trucks, chairs and animals. My raspy throat, dry like sandpaper, craved constant water, any moisture.

Those first years of fire season caught us completely off guard. I felt so small standing next to it. If you haven't been near a fire, you cannot imagine the force of it. I felt tiny, infinitesimal, surrounded by its hot orange, ripping power, swooping with ferocious speed, over our once lush hillsides. It's incomprehensible agony. Friends walked through ash where their comfy homes once were, looking for a wedding ring, a photo, toys, pet birds, cats' bodies, anything that resembled their former lives.

Cass stumbled to the kitchen to fill the animals water bowls. I wobbled across the street, in my bathrobe, hoping for reassurance, to talk to a firefighter neighbor of thirty years. He groaned trying to take off his heavy, rubbery overalls. I'd never seen his face swollen like that, his cheeks beet red, bloated, his eyes riveted on mine.

Tom is a big, sturdy, solid vocal guy about six feet tall, maybe two hundred pounds. But on this day, his words were labored, hardly uttered from his parched mouth, "In thirty years of doing this, I've never seen anything like it." His chest sunk, emptying breath, then swelled, grasping for rare air: "I ran from the flames, the winds caught us off guard, fire from every direction. When I turned my head, fire was grabbing at my heels." He whispered he'd never seen anything like it in all his years of firefighting. He quietly turned, closing the door. I knew he had seen death up close.

It's a myth that women's friendships are easy. When wounds run deep, we explode like pressure-sensitive landmines, dangerous to step on.

There are no words for this kind of terror.

I stood in the empty street. Sonoma was like a ghost town now with everyone evacuating.

Inside the house Cassandra chain smoked cigarettes. It didn't matter, smoke was everywhere anyway. Panicked, she wandered through the patio and kitchen nervously, the animals trailing behind her, plunking paws on the wood floors. The shortest pooch was worn out, faded grey hair, shuffling slowly. The other one about hip high, with a wise stare, charcoal, wearing a darling white beard, a kind dog. She picked up the old, beige dachshund, cuddling him to her chest. The shivering black cat, sat silently inside at the back corner of the big wire carrier, glazed eyes, petrified like a stone.

The Tubbs fire was one of the fiercest near our usually

serene county. Hot, blazing commanding flames jumped a solid concrete freeway, grasping mountains and homes in its vicious claws, devouring deer, squirrels, and fields, leaving charred, grieving earth.

Shrieking sirens surrounded our scorched neighborhoods. Friends sped by me in their big vans, packed to the brim, with sleeping bags, kids and clothing bulging out of back seats, dog ears flying out their windows. They barely said good bye. I thought my neighbors cared more about me. But crisis tells all. Had I not reached out enough to them over the years?

Bullhorns blared in our ears, perforating our eardrums. Numb, zombie like, this kind of terror anesthetizes you. California was on fire.

The next morning, disheveled, looking mummified and bleary eyed we walked into the chaotic kitchen full of sandwich wrappers, cigarette butts, dog food and plastic water bottles. I could hardly hear her voice: "I'd like to stay one more night but I want you to know it's okay to say *no*."

My legs trembling, I mumbled, "I think I need a break." In an instant, she plunked down her coffee, corralling the black cat. She sped through the house, like lightning, grabbing her animals. Then, in a whisk of an unexpected moment, she barreled away.

I didn't hear from Cassandra for a year. I tried to call her three or four times, leaving desperate messages, "let's talk about what happened." I finally gave up.

It's a myth that women's friendships are easy. When wounds run deep, we explode like pressure-sensitive land-mines, dangerous to step on. *No* is a dangerous word. Daniel

Yankelovich wrote it well in, *The Magic of Dialogue*, "My friend's assertion that dialogue is as simple as chewing gum is dead wrong. Chewing gum is simple; it is both easy to understand and easy to do. Dialogue is neither easy to understand, not easy to do." It's excruciatingly hard because an untreated hurt, like an infection, festers. Our being becomes impacted. The decay creates disease between us, inside us and in our communities.

Time passed, as time tends to do. Then I ran into her at the grocery store. There she stood. Both of us barely holding onto our bags of bread and fruit, shocked to see each other, we bantered a few awkward words. I asked if she would call me and she agreed.

When the phone finally rang, my heart pounded, protruding right out of my chest. I stared at her name on my cell phone. It was one of those moments, the kind we all know – you start to sweat.

Seconds seemed like hours. All my tools about skilled communication went vamoose, skedaddled, disappeared as fast as people fleeing the fire. I blithered a few words, "I feel badly that we haven't talked."

The language of empathy in communication is not intrinsic in us. We are pioneering it. When you're standing in that kind of fire –the fire of conflict, you can't research or google how to deal with it. Even with all my years of studying the art of difficult dialogue, I forgot how to "do it." It seemed too steep a mountain. And that's exactly what it's like, it takes everything you've got. Your mind races for ways to approach the gutsy conversation.

We women are just as challenged as men at managing

our reactivity. It's a myth that women have less anger than men, in my experience. We've just learned to be coy or clawing like angry cats, then retreating to gossip or stonewalling. One study by Ruber and Raquel Gur found that while the amygdala is a similar size in men and women, a second region, called the orbital frontal cortex, which is involved in controlling aggressive impulses, is much larger in women. They suggest this could help explain why women seem to be better at keeping the lid on explosive outbursts. (University of Pennsylvania School of Medicine / British Guardian 5/12/2019, Hannah Devlin, *Anger: Users Guide / Science of Anger*)

She wanted me to say yes because I cared, not because I had to

How many days I had wondered why she disappeared. Was it all my fault? Was it hers? Was I expecting too much? Why couldn't she just call me to talk it through? Now I worried that this conversation could go ballistic. You never know for sure.

She blurted out, "I felt so betrayed."

Finally, implanted memory reminded me of my tools for communication. Keep listening, I told myself, don't interrupt, just make "I" statements. Those little reminders can save my ass.

"I'm not sure why I was afraid to call you," she said. This is exactly how it goes sometimes, we don't know why we respond in certain ways, we have to guess.

I hesitated, walking on eggshells, as I stated my intention. "I wish we could work this through." Saying your intention always helps lubricate the dialogue.

She said her fear was that she would not be understood. She worried that I might argue with her and not respect her feelings. For a year, she'd imagined herself in a confrontation, with me debating her viewpoint. It really is like unwinding a ball of yarn. She bravely admitted that she had never felt heard growing up, saying, "I had to be tough. My needs never mattered."

We had an old pattern, she shut down, stonewalling after conflicts. I floundered with anxiety. I would pry her out of hiding, we'd talk and things would be okay for a while.

I told her how, on the day she left I was confused. A part of me wanted to be there for her and another part was shaken from fatigue and constant cortisol coursing through me. I craved even a shred of quiet solitude, but I was ashamed – afraid of being selfish. *I always know I'm telling the truth if I feel embarrassed.*

Self-investigation isn't always easy; we have to guess at what we feel until it resonates with us.

I confessed, "when you said, 'It's alright if you say no', I thought you meant it." My heart throbbing through my chest, I knew combustion could come at any second. I was afraid of throwing a match to another kind of flame. It just takes a spark to start a fire.

It turned out, what she meant was she wanted me to say yes because I cared, not because I had to. Yes and No are treacherous territory in relationships. We want connection. We're afraid of suffocation but terrified of abandonment.

_____

"When another person is talking, you want to be listening so actively that you're practically burning calories."

– David Brooks

_____

69

Our guesswork seemed to help. She realized that asking for what she needed made her feel silly, even pitiful. I talked about how I was always petrified of my mom's anger, stating my wants or even identifying them threatening to our attachment.

How many hours do we humans spend in our heads having the conversations we avoid?

Cassandra offered her soft underbelly, "Mostly I don't call because I'm unsure of what to say and afraid," pause . . . "I don't know how to have these conversations. I just kept going round and round in my head wondering what I would say."

Listening is like going through labor. It's crucial not to interrupt with our immediate rebuttal. It's a reflex to defend our perspective. David Brooks writes, "When another person is talking, you want to be listening so actively that you're practically burning calories." (*How to Know a Person*)

Communication during conflict mimics moving through a birth canal. You hope to God you come out alive and loved. I held my hand to my heart. Sometimes it helps me remember to just listen and let the other person unfold. She was "going down the ladder" – lowering herself, into her deeper self – an act of courage.

How many hours do we humans spend in our heads having the conversations we avoid?

Author Barry Lopez said, "You can't gain intimacy without vulnerability . . . Part of our difficulty is that we have trouble trusting people, so we rarely get to the place where we can open up . . . There's a wall we can't get through." He adds, "that lack of intimacy and vulnerability in human culture is manifesting in a lack of intimacy with the land. Those two feed each other." (Interview in The Sun Magazine, Dec. 2019)

Our cumbersome conversation gave me courage. I said what I wished for, though I thought it might be impossible. "What I want – is to keep our relationship, but not so close as before. I love you and would like to have lunch once in awhile or talk, but I don't want to get so close that I risk going through this cycle anymore. The panic attacks I get when you're angry, and then you shut down for days – are tough on me. (My mother's rage had left their mark. I'm now hyper sensitive to unexpected anger.)

Lack of intimacy and vulnerability in human culture is manifesting in a lack of intimacy with the land. Those two feed each other.

"Well, that makes me feel abandoned again," she was hurting again. Oh God, this was not going well.

Groping for words, asking for what we want is hard. It's challenging to identify, let alone saying it out loud. "I need less anxiety in my aging years. I walk on eggshells when you're mad."

(It's always hardest to identify our own issues – not judging the other.)

Cassandra's survival strategy was to disappear, seeking solace in separation from an abusive dad. I was soothed by safe communication, reassured by it. Her attachment style was "avoidant." Mine was anxious.

Repair happened. By going through it we were actually

telling our own parents, "here is what I need." Weeks later, back at the grocery store, I ran into Cassandra again. Flooded with trepidation, I stiffened, would she be mad after that demanding conversation?

She beamed, "I love you." It was like giving birth! The triumph that comes from hard work! And as I write this, we just got off the phone! We enjoy staying in touch.

Cass and I knitted a piece of community back together. Metamorphosis can be slow growth. But, it's miraculous to work through difficulties and discover new life on the other side of the ominous birth canal.

This process of moving from conflict to communication heals us, makes us whole. "Humanity is growing up. We are in our adolescence as a human family." (*A New Republic of the Heart*, Terry Patten quoting Duane Elgin)

We are all a thread in the giant web of this world. Cassandra and I made choices along the way. The passage was mysterious, scary sometimes, not knowing how to change and reconstruct our relationship. *What matters is that we still sustain the web.*

BOUNDARIES ARE A SUBSTITUTE FOR THE SOUL

In the end Mom taught me: Why Walls Don't Work

Sometimes you stop speaking to someone for years, or you pull back. It's an unnecessary loss. Mom and I did not know how to talk through our hidden hurt. Oh, there were the friendly phone calls, the polite and brief conversations, but something was missing. *It's not always the things we say to each other that destroy our relationships. It's sometimes the things unsaid that sever them.* Words that sit like stale, unspoken resentments or fears reside inside and between us, in the thick space of silences that kill connection.

While it may be true that we can't change others we can be brave ourselves and attempt repair and closure

When my mother died I fell into a killing field of unsaid words. Her suicide smashed my nose right up against a closed window in a cold winter. We lost a precious opportunity to communicate because I detached from her. We could have reached each other, if we had walked through our fears and talked. I kept my distance. I had "boundaries." It was wrong.

I started removing myself from Mom, bit by bit. I thought that "setting boundaries" was healthy. But it was another wall. I left our visits without telling her my feelings or wishes. I suppressed my longings. I had learned to detach and let her vent. So, I limited our phone calls. I believed it was useless to try, she wouldn't hear me, she was too difficult. But I did not take responsibility for trying to be heard. I could have reached across the crevasse with curiosity.

I assumed she was too difficult to approach, that she was the problem, and that ignoring her or "doing my own thing," was the way to be healthy. It wasn't.

Self-sufficiency was what we had both learned. We did need to become interdependent, but distancing was not life giving.

Separating from our mothers can be a part of growing up. Written so well, in *Between Women* "the feelings between them can become so intense, the need for one another so strong, and the transferences so deep, that it can feel too threatening to bring up difficulties." Differentiating is challenging, but another divide or crevasse is not what we need – it's equally important to keep authentic connections. (Eichenbaum and Orbach)

I was afraid to say things I thought might hurt her. I learned in therapy that boundaries were good. So, I withdrew before she died.

As she aged, she got angrier and I shut down. I was afraid of her outbursts and criticisms. It didn't occur to me to tell her that. I thought: "you can't change people," "don't rock the boat" or "I don't want to hurt her or fight." While it may be true that we can't change others we can be brave ourselves and attempt repair and closure.

I left my trips to see her from San Francisco to Seattle, in a hurry. After one of those visits, she killed herself.

It was a cold night arriving back in Seattle to her empty apartment. The neighbors discovered newspapers mounting up on the doorstep, so they called the police. I pleaded with the funeral home to see her one more time, but they said I wouldn't want to. Alone, I entered the house with trepidation, a haunted feeling. I tip toed, like some kind of silent secrecy surrounded me. Where was she? Maybe there was a mistake. I was in incredible shock.

I found blood at the edge of her bed, on her bedroom rug. She had emphysema, so she must have tried to catch her breath, after taking the drugs and bent over the bed to gasp for breath. She probably tried to lay down, to let go, but couldn't. She left pills next to the bed, (knowing her), so that I knew how she did it. It must have been a struggle at the end to breathe. They said she was in warm, flannel pajamas, so I knew they were the ones I had given her for Christmas.

It's not always the things we say to each other that destroy our relationships. It's sometimes the things unsaid that sever them.

It was clearly carefully planned.

I scoured the house, picking up towels and blankets, desperately searching her clothing. I knew mom wouldn't leave me without some words. And there, hidden underneath a towel in the kitchen, I found a few little notes she must have written as she wandered around . . . her hand writing gradually shriveling from fuzzy to fading . . . saying things like, "don't feel guilty, you were a good daughter. My body is tired." That one note stayed with me all my life: "don't feel guilty . . . " it's helped me through. She scribbled, in her own frisky way: "I enjoyed life, especially my little Toyota, but my body is finished." Oddly, it took days for me to find all her handwritten hidden notes scattered around the house.

Our attachment was tempestuous, smothering and tender. Our bond fiery and fun. My mother was a fighter for fairness and the common good. But she had a divide inside. We swapped ideas, opinions and ardent writing, giddy during shopping trips for clothes, bartering jokes, talking excitably after drowning in frustrated repartee about politics. We both loved to write.

We hid our judgments of each other, grimacing inside ourselves about each others edgy and difficult characteristics. (When we're afraid of telling the truth, we focus on the faults of others.) She was controlling, pushing me to think the same way she did. I was moody and hard to understand half the time. We were too much alike, the way mothers and daughters can be.

On the night she died, I sat by my phone, at my desk, in unusual quiet. I rarely did that. I started saying the serenity prayer, out loud. The telephone rang. It was about 7 pm. I remember it well because I looked at the clock. I wondered if it was a mistaken call, with nobody on the other end because she paused so long. It was a thick space, one of those moments in time that stay lodged in us forever. It was unlike her to not fill the silent void – or even to call at that hour. Then came her sullen, meditative words, in blunt contrast to her usual bold voice. She uttered, "Oh, you usually don't talk around this hour." She was right. I was always at dinner with my husband at that time. But that night, my chair felt like a suction cup. I stammered, "I know. I am just praying." Praying was something I rarely did.

She asked, "what prayer?" I read it to her: "God, grant me the serenity to accept the things I cannot change, the courage to change the things I can and the wisdom to know the difference." Then there was quiet space, each of us saying, shyly: "I love you."

That same night, at 11 pm – I remember that exact time very well, because I was so disturbed, I glanced

You can't gain intimacy without vulnerability

at the clock. My body seemed to take over in a way I have never experienced before. I sobbed, my shoulders shook. I had never done anything like this for no apparent reason. I woke up my husband.

"Something is happening under my skin, like a tidal wave. I don't know what it is. I can't stop crying." Uncontrollable tremors ran through my entire body. I thought I was crazy. Richard held me for a long time until we both fell asleep.

The next morning, I phoned mom as soon as I woke up. I called three times and each time a strange, deep voiced man answered, so I hung up. I thought I'd misdialed. On the third call, I knew it was her home number. He mumbled in a low, garbled tone, "hello." Beseechingly I begged, "Is my mother there?" And that was another long quiet moment, then he stated flatly, "Yes, she's here." Relieved, yearning, I thought maybe she had just taken a fall or something, "Oh, can I talk to her?" Another choking pause.

"No, she's dead."

The world fell in and along with it the impossible, contrasting, strange and burdensome tasks of packing her things. Engulfed with selling, signing documents and in shock, I was horrified with my first experience at a funeral "parlor."

The staff were white-faced. They walked toward me down a long, white corridor, like slithering, dusty ghosts. I remember wondering if the continual cremations in the basement, the fire burning furnaces had left residue sunken into them. It was surreal and lonely beyond anyone's ability to describe, unless you've gone through it. Standing there, shattered – in an altered state – in unbearable sorrow alongside these contrasting robot-like, bony, cold humans.

I was taught to have "boundaries" so I withdrew and became devoid of feeling

It might seem like an odd insert here, but this writing is suddenly too hard. My mind darts around, boggled, looking for ways to tell you what it was like. I'm feeling inadequate for what this story wants me to convey. But, I will try. I often flash on quotes or stories when I'm stuck. I remember something the great correspondent, Ed Murrow struggled to convey after seeing atrocities at Nazi concentration camps, "I pray you believe what I have said. I reported what I saw and heard, but only part of it. For most of it I have no words."

Some experiences are not of this world. These strange,

cadaver like people kept asking me formal, impersonal questions. He wore a tie that looked more like a noose, and a compact charcoal suit. She stood tense in an anorexic body, taut dress, stiff, narrow, pointed high heels. It's odd how vivid this memory remains while so many other details are lost.

I finally walked out of the "funeral home" for dead people. I returned to my parent's apartment, with vacant rooms, the furniture sold, my favorite art in the U haul and one phone, a landline, sitting on the floor, with a wire still connected to the wall. Dad had passed two years earlier of lymphatic cancer. It was desolate in the "living room," no pillows, no paintings, no furniture, no music or television, only stone white walls. I waited for the realtor, to sign more impersonal paperwork. Mom and I seemed to be traveling an ethereal, solitary tunnel alone but still together. Somehow, in space, I seemed to be walking through death with her, still without words.

It's a myth that boundaries make us safe. They leave us empty.

I sat on the rug, staring at the empty home of my upbringing. That place where so much life has been, holidays with hilarity and arguments, my brother and father in a flurry of fast flying wit, mom, an inborn Irish humorist. The aroma of her chocolate chip cookies – cookies we waited for each holiday, and ravenously devoured too soon.

What I would give to have been brave enough to talk to her about unspoken feelings before she died. We think we have forever for this, but we don't. Closure is a gift we give ourselves.

If only I had the courage to say: "Mom, I want to feel closer to you" or "I get afraid around your rage." Instead, I withdrew and became devoid of feeling, devouring cookies. Never taught to ask for what we want, walls and isolation remain a result. *Boundaries are a substitute for soul* – spaces separating our deep selves and longings.

I can only guess she was scared of being a burden at the end. And I had trepidation about telling her my mixed emotions about caregiving for her. Those feelings remain in the dust. If we could have had a conversation about how she felt about being alone with emphysema, getting into ambulances at midnight in the rain by herself. If I had shared my concerns about how to be there for her while still trying to keep my own life functioning, we might have shared the struggle.

We need to break out of our self-suffocating digital privacy bubbles and engage with the people around us, even when our default is to put on our headphones and scroll on our phones.

– Noreena Hertz

It's a myth that boundaries make us safe. They leave us empty. They may be needed under duress, when harm is threatened or we feel too fragile to try to bridge divides. Yet, mostly what the soul does is yearn. Whether it's walls, technology, or AI, we're not meant to be so alone.

"We need to break out of our self-suffocating digital privacy bubbles and engage with the people around us, even when our default is to put on our headphones and scroll on our phones." (*The Lonely Century*, Noreena Hertz)

Trying to put back together my split apart heart, I wrote to my mother, my aching reparation:

Dearest Mom,

If you can hear me, I want you to know, more than anything, I was afraid. I was terrified you wouldn't listen. I didn't want to leave, but I was scared of making it worse, saying the wrong thing, having a fight, so I said nothing.

Most of all, I couldn't tell you what I felt. I wanted you to hear my needs too.

I couldn't find a way to talk about death, about dad being gone, about our relationship. I didn't know how to be vulnerable. I was scared to tell you what I needed. I didn't listen.

I love you.
Katy

If I had known how to tell the truth, we might have mended our divide.

HOW TO DO IT?

How to have Gutsy Conversations

When we enter difficult dialogues, we need something to help us, to hold onto, like an inner tube or lifesaver as we go into deep waters. Here is my suggested support and scaffolding for the necessary conversations facing our future (there is more explanation at the back of the book):

When we start a sticky dialogue we're more wired and upset than usual. So, I've made the "how to have crucial conversations" easy to remember. One of my clients calls it "rules of war" or I sometimes refer to it as "cliff notes" for conflict. There are three simple tools.

When we're upset, we need to lean on a calm and helpful person or structure (in psychology we call this 'object constancy.')
"At those times, the brain is in a state in which the pre-frontal cortex is neither connected to nor soothing the sub-cortical system – 'us' evaporates and becomes you and me, adversaries in a cold world of 'I win, you lose.'" (*Us* by Terrence Real)

Resentment is rooted in unmet needs.

So, I build delicate dialogue around the image of a face: the eyes, ears and mouth (ears for listening.) It's easy to remember because you are looking at their face! And you're saving face!

We have two eyes. The first **eye** begins the deliberate dialogue with an "I" – for stating your intention – your aim, the outcome you want. "I would like to work this through," or "I want to enjoy our time together," or "I want to communicate better," etc. (Some prefer "we" statements, but for disputes, I will explain why the *eye* is more important for the main thrust of difficult dialogue.)

The *"I"* is from word *INTENTION. It is profoundly powerful.* It's why you hear amazing rescue stories from people with sincere, intense intentions.

Repeat your intention in the conversation, often – it sets the tone. It leads us to the light at the end of the tunnel: "I want to leave this job on good terms" or "I wish we could remain friends." A positive intention or vision soothes, centers and lowers the temperature in the room. It en-

The act of asking –

for what you wish for –

also supports the other

person to stretch, to

change and grow.

courages suspension of judgement. An intention holds the space with more calm. *It holds hope. It's like walking toward the lake with a picnic basket knowing at the end of the road, we'll feel better.*

The other "eye" – is the "I" that states your feelings, your needs, fears or hurt. "I feel rejected when you don't call." Or "I get scared when you drive so fast. "These words open up investigation into your own self. What makes you feel that way? Is there a past memory of something similar that hurt you, etc.? The "I", or eye, forces self-reflection. It builds connection with others because you are revealing yourself — offering a way to feel known.

The reason YOU statements don't work is they always imply a criticism. Even the word YOU quickly makes the hair stand up on your back like a cat waiting for a fight. The immense problem with YOU is it pulls us away from our own embodied feelings. Can YOU even feel it's punch reading the word? It puts everyone in rebuttal mode, thinking of their own self-defenses.

The "I" is the eye of the soul . . . it's for learning about yourself and letting others see you. That's why we avoid it. It makes us vulnerable. But, it's also essential for connectivity. Ironically, in partner-dancing you have to be on your own two feet and to be totally attuned to your partner. "We" emerges from two separate selves. You have to stay tuned to yourself and the other simultaneously.

The **mouth** is for asking for our **wishes** or for our request. It's like making a wish and blowing candles off a birthday cake. When you say requests, especially doable ones, it is a way to direct your anger. *Resentment is rooted in unmet needs.*

Be aware, asking for what you want is not as easy as it sounds. It's not just the surface request, like "I wish you would pick up your laundry." It's ideally a deeper want, like "I'm less anxious when the house is organized. It helps me feel centered." *When you explain your wish, it gives the request a context so your partner or collaborator understands it. The explanation* gives the conversation a heart, then it's less likely to be experienced as a demand.

Asking can be harder than it seems. It makes us feel bare, our shields stolen. Asking doesn't insure that we'll get what we want, but we feel sturdier because we stood in our request. It's essential. People aren't psychic, they will not know what you need unless you tell them. So, the act of asking – for what you wish for – also supports the other person to stretch, to change and grow.

The ears are for listening, engrossed listening, leaning with empathy into what others feel, *getting out of your own head*. It is imperative to listen closely for their feelings under their words. Just listening for facts and reporting what you heard will not bring connection. There is a space around words that tells you what emotions are there . . . listen for them. **This is important.** Research shows that the average person listens at about 25% efficiency." (Wright State University Education)

"A good conversation is a joint act of joint exploration."

– David Brooks

"Everyone in a conversation is facing an internal conflict between self expression and self inhibition," writes David Brooks. For a remedy, the feeling quality of the problem has to be named, for instance, *"I hear you saying you feel lonely, disconnected from the staff, . . . did I get that right? Is there more?"* Clients tell me that when the emotion behind their words is reflected back to them, they feel heard in a new way. (*How to Know a Person*, Brooks)

Witnessing individuals in deep dialogue reminds me of people afraid they are about to be beheaded, but instead they end up on an altar – bowing in an act of honor. By reflecting back what they hear each other saying they feel closer. "What I hear you saying is that you hoped to celebrate your wedding anniversary because it *made you feel like you matter*. Did I hear that right?" The person you are mirroring can let you know if you missed something that matters to them. Listening is a bigger deal than we know – because the brain only hears half of what it takes in. In most learning – "within one-hour people have forgotten an average of 50% of the information. In 24-hours they have forgotten an average of 70% of the new information." (Learning Guild/ Brain Science/ 2014).

I have to stop people often and slow them down to listen. The urge to jump in to defend ourselves is an enemy – claws want to come out. We argue too soon and destroy the listening. If all else fails, keep going back to repeating the hope or intention – it soothes everyone, like turning down the heat on a boiling pot: "I'm hoping to respect each other's point of view or find solutions that work for us all."

_____

The "I" is the eye of the soul. It's for learning about yourself and letting others see you. That's why we avoid it. It makes us vulnerable.

_____

Slow the dialogue down. The rhythm of it is like eating when you're less uptight, *it makes better digestion. Saying your first truth first, let it sink in, and be heard.* Put your toe in the water before you dive in. The average person speaks at a rate of about 120 – 150 words a minute. The speed of it alone sparks argument.

I will often start contentious counseling with their wishes – what is their hoped for outcome? It helps people see the end goal, the joy of it. I'll repeat it so we all absorb it: "Your aim or desire here is to renew the enjoyment you had for each other in your early marriage." It's important that the intention is sincere, visceral, a felt image. It's like painting a vivid, pleasing picture – *it can leave an imprint, a map – for the trip ahead.* Studies show images are remembered best, subjects are significantly more able to recall items that are *presented as pictures.*

When clients freeze or get confused, I suggest more "I" statements, rather than "you are rude and a bully . . ." It could be "the story in my head is that you are going to be critical of me whenever I come home from work."

These tools lubricate good listening and understanding. "I'd argue that we have become so sad, lonely, angry and mean as a society in part because so many people have not been taught or don't bother practicing to enter sympathetically into the minds of their fellow human beings." (*The New York Times*, Jan 28, 2024, David Brooks.) We shun or gossip with indirect criticisms, another slice of violence – instead of braving difficult dialogue.

We need deliberate time set aside for these conversations. I'll explain helpful ways to move through conflict more clearly at the end of the book.

DENIAL AND SHUTTING DOWN RUNS DEEP

There was a day when I mustered every ounce of strength I had and told my parents the truth. Monica Guzman writes, "Curiosity is worthless without honesty. If people hold back in conversation, release little, put on a mask, is anyone really learning?" (*I Never Thought of it That Way*)

I told mom she had yelled and criticized too much after her cocktails every night. She immediately, of course, denied it in full living color. To her this movie I was running was far afield from her reality. Then I asked my father why he had allowed it. I mustered every ounce of courage and moved past my anxiety about hurting him long enough to say that I believed his denial of her rage and criticisms had done harm to me as a now – too insecure and anxious adult and had disabled my brother in

> *"Curiosity is worthless without honesty. If people hold back in conversation, release little, put on a mask, is anyone really learning?"*
>
> – Monica Guzman

too many ways. My father sobbed uncontrollably for the only time I had seen that in my life. His shoulders shook as he sobbed at the dinner table, holding his head down in his hand.

The depth of denial, compartmentalization and dissociation from old habits goes deep – like being rooted in the most ancient tree.

That was a horrible night. Mom poured another drink screaming at me for making up such lies, as she had always done. It had confused me for too many years. Making me not trust my own opinions or reality and even now, I still doubt myself. "Who do I think I am? How could I think that? Maybe I'm wrong."

After that she quit drinking until the last day of her life. It was hard on my dad, drinking at night was their ritual, though he never imbibed too much.

The funny thing is, maybe not so funny, is that a couple of years later Dad and I took a walk alone together, a rare happening. I asked him how he felt after all that and how he viewed moms constant anger, which still happened, even now without booze, she remained a dry drunk – which means she never went to AA or therapy, so the anger, in her case, still resided over the living room every night, even while drinking tea. He said the same thing he always did, "She can't help it. She has emphysema."

His denial was too deep. He lied to himself. That's how entrenched was Dad's need for belonging. Growing up, not feeling loved, in a group of 12 siblings, Mom was his main relationship. He clung to her like a child holding on to a cold, wire monkey, just like in the studies by Harlow of monkeys given fake, emotionally unavailable mothers. They still clung to them, even though there was no warmth or nurturing. This was all they knew. (Association for Psychology, June 20, 2018)

Our defenses are carved into us, our way to survive. I often need to interpret defenses in my clients in order to help them relate better. Some are unfeeling workaholics or sticky sweet backstabbers – overly intellectualized or belligerent. There are a thousand defense strategies, sometimes subtle, but once we verbalize them we realize we made it hard for others to get close to us.

My dad hid behind his overly-adaptive, polite demeanor. He meant well, but his passivity enabled Mom's aggression.

Just so you know, I do regret the way I told the truth that day. I wasn't skilled enough then. It's best to have more tools to help dignify difficult dialogues.

DIVORCE

The Long Road to Repair

Lessons that arrive too late are still lessons. Like what I learned in my marriage starting out in two years of bliss ending in a long slope to hell. Ted had few communication skills and I was still developing mine. At first, everything was calm and exciting with lots of sex, socializing and giggling. As time went by our dark sides swelled, spiraling around us. Challenges with finance and work overwhelmed us while we struggled with our reactions.

He appeared so mellow and flexible in the beginning, with humor galore. I liked his family and friends. But, as our shadows erupted, I either blustered around in anger or cried myself to sleep. He withdrew or screamed.

Powerless to recapture the innocence and love of our early years, we separated. After all the drama that comes with spikes of emotion — we splintered and crawled up in separate spaces. His family distrusted me, wondering if I was the demon that brought it all on.

His brother and I exchanged awful emails, technology got us nowhere. I called a divorce mediator and there we went. Ted and I and the two dogs trailing behind me, into his office, week after week. We hoped for a fair resolution to money matters. The discussions went on and on, circular, going nowhere. In fact, the "arbitrator" became distracted and enthralled with Teds artistic side. So, they spent half of our "sessions" sharing tips on art.

I was so tired, in a battle against him and his entire family. I sat one day and realized there was nobody to save me.

It's odd how crystal clear certain words and memories remain, while so much else is a blur.

In silence, checking my gut. I was completely ragged, crumbling, done in, spent, walking at half my height, back bent over like a wobbly old lady at 45. I had to pull up some strength, from somewhere. I searched my insides. All I could find there was my genuine intention.

I walked, war torn, with the little dogs getting as tangled up in their leashes as we were – into the last session with that divorce negotiator. After dozens of meetings, I opened my mouth "I have decided I don't want any money if it has to be a fight. I'm exhausted. I want to be an honest, ethical person. All I want is fairness and closure to a marriage that mattered to me." Using my "I" statements and intentions, I started to stand up.

Weak and about to walk away, something unexpected happened. The mediator changed his demeanor, putting on his big leather cowboy hat, lowering his tone, puffing his feathers. Gargling a cough, bristling his shoulders upright, he sat taller. Turning his chair to stare at Ted, he suddenly boomed in a bold voice, "Well, I guess I'll have to put on my lawyer hat then. Now I must tell your husband that if he doesn't settle and give you something financially, any judge in a court of law will insist on a great deal more than what you are asking for here." And that was that. We found a fair decision.

It's odd how crystal clear certain words and memories remain, while so much else is a blur. His words came as a shock. Then I nervously searched myself again. How could I find closure with his family? It was still ugly between us. I put my hand on my gut. I was frail from fear, but I found a tiny belief inside, still believing in intention. So I wrote his brother asking that we find a way to hear each other and find peace. The exchange of emails went nowhere, they were the usual swapping of facts that always rule arguments – what you did, etc. Then, I asked for my most true wish – friendship and fairness.

Another surprise – Ted's brother suggested handwritten notes, saying he felt that might help him get closer to his feelings. And that was that. We found a higher ground of caring about the common good, through only a couple of letters.

Years later we even became a helpful team when my "ex" was very ill and almost died. We all survived it and were revived. This is what can unfold with authentic dialogue. But, attachments aren't always that simple to say good-by to. Twenty years later we're still good friends though we still get triggered, communication is much more fluid and fun. "Continuing bonds can be a part of normal grief," says Pauline Boss, Ph.D. (*Ambiguous Loss and the Myth of Closure*)

I even tremble a little writing this, just because tonight I go out for dinner with Ted, his brother and his wife. It's hard to explain how I feel reliving the pain of those years. Still, I'm also realizing what can unfold with voicing a higher intention. It's been a hard lesson, but the rewards that arrive when we

move from conflict to communication are so much more satis-
fying. It's been twenty years since that crucible. We're actually
going to dinner tonight, for fun.

WHEN TO HOLD 'EM
WHEN TO FOLD 'EM

When to Leave?

Working through conflict is like going to the dentist. We simply have to do it or keep destroying the fabric of our lives. Is there a time to give up though?

I am often asked "how do we know when to leave or when to hold 'em?" I always smile because we all hope someone will tell us an easy answer. It's a valid question. There are times to say "no." When there is a possible threat to oneself or others. Also, when you are just not up to the task. It is a choice and sometimes we don't feel well enough, strong enough or able. *It takes courage* but also psychic, physical energy and some skill to "hold 'em and work through difficulties.

As Erin Brockovich, famous environmental legal researcher wrote, "Sometimes the real and only victory is knowing when to walk away." Our decade encourages cell phones, texts, basically technology – not human connection. It's a dangerous temptation to text or quit responding. But, *my bias is that most of us already do plenty of that*. I believe building bridges, not walls – is the most imperative work we have to do.

It is harder than walking away, that's why we don't do it. But I repeat, do not risk harm to yourself or to others. (*Take It from Me,* Brockovich and Eliot)

Extending ourselves, reaching across a crevasse is boggling, but urgent – if we want to evolve as a species. At this pivotal point we have one group pitted against the other wherever we turn. We have complex crises, like climate change and nuclear threats among others.

> *"Sometimes the real and only victory is knowing when to walk away."*
>
> – Erin Brockovich

I believe that the biggest lessons occur when each of us stretches, doing "radical reaching out." Rather than pulling back from life – *we contribute and strengthen the world web.* As Jeremy Lent eloquently explains: "Each of us has a part to play in weaving that web of vital synergy . . . Like an immune system protecting its host from toxins." (*The Web of Meaning.*) I saw how this works, just this week, when a woman phoned to thank me for the columns I write in *The Sonoma Sun.* Her call perked me up like a double latte, while I shuffled a desk full of challenging tasks. While we chatted, I suggested a coffee date. She mentioned another woman that might be a charming addition. Imagine if all of us were doing this. Just one phone call led to three rejuvenated people. We are electrical currents. We generate goodwill by extending ourselves.

It's going to take a conviction and a thrust away from self-involvement, towards "the power of the people" and erasing fear of "the other." As Barry Lopez said, "We need new narratives at the center of which is a concern for the fate of all people. The story can't continue to be adoration of one leader. It has to be about the heroism of communities." (*The Sun Magazine* / 12/2019 / interview Fred Bahnson)

This exact idea could be accomplished between countries and politicians. Simply listening to each other without sarcasm. Closeness comes from crucial conversations done well. In John F Kennedy's *Peace Speech*, he describes peace "as the necessary rational end [goal] of rational men." Yet he acknowledges: "I realize that the pursuit of peace is not as dramatic as the pursuit of war — and frequently the words of the pursuer fall on deaf ears. But we have no more urgent task."

It is easy to fall into the trap of blaming, warns Kennedy. "We must reexamine our own attitude—as individuals and as a Nation—for our attitude is as essential as theirs."

He attacked prevailing pessimism about the necessity of battle, "that war is inevitable—that mankind is doomed—that we are gripped by forces we cannot control. We need not accept that view. Our problems are man-made—therefore, they can be solved by man." Said Kennedy, we must not "see conflict as inevitable, accommodation as impossible, and communication as nothing more than an exchange of threats." (June 10, 1963)

We generate goodwill by extending ourselves.

Our world is approaching global death on every level . . . economics, climate, hunger, migration, the end of animal life, etc. As Barry Lopez explained, "Our existence relies on a fundamental pivot in our psychological collective psyche." He elaborates: "We need new narratives at the center of which is concern for the fate of all people. The story can't be about the heroism of one person. It has to be about the heroism of communities." It's time to steer the globe away from the great lie of individuality. We really can't afford to minimize the importance of keeping our connections in divided communities.

We all long for belonging.

When facilitators are generally devoted to dignity, not shaming, criticizing, or over-advising based on their own ego needs, then many people, credentialed or not, can be capable. We don't need more professionals on pedestals like Dr. Oz. (I want to be clear, training matters but more so does devotion.)

Gabor Mate writes in *The Myth of Normal* . . . "chronic negation of one's authentic experience can be fatal." In a study that followed nearly two thousand women over ten years, those "who reported that, in conflict with their spouses, they usually or always kept their feelings to themselves, had over four times the risk of dying during the follow-up compared with women who always showed their feelings."

According to *Bowling Alone*, by Robert Putnam, when asked whether "most people can be trusted" 55% surveyed in 1960 thought they could. Asked the same questions in the 80's and 90's the number fell to around 35%. (Capita/ Ian Marcus Corbin) One in two people say they don't know their neighbors. (Forbes Oct. 24, 2013.) I'm not going to belabor statistics here, we all know the divorce rate is high (74% for third marriages (1/1/2023 The Micklin Law Group)

In order to keep knitting our world together deciding to end relationships should be carefully examined. We are too quick to create endings.

We are conditioned by childhood and culture. As one of my clients said this week, while exploring her own reactions, wanting to change the way she is too critical with her husband, a lot like her mother, "Are there ways we swallow our parents whole?" Yes, we do. Gabor Maté writes: "Traumatic childhood experiences have been shown to bear very directly on adult political orientations." We've learned prejudice and breaking things – it's time to repair instead and reach out. Michael Milburn, emeritus professor of psychology at the University of Massachusetts, found that the harsher the parenting people were exposed to as young children, the more prone they become to support authoritarian or aggressive policies, such as foreign wars, punitive laws, and the death penalty. Maté adds, "surely social maladies like addiction and global catastrophes like climate change are all signs of something amiss in the body politic."

In order to change the killing fields and separations as Richard Harwood wrote, "When we do not go together as communities, we remain divided and fragmented. Loneliness becomes inevitable. Challenges mount and begin to look intractable . . . Yet, all too often, we withdraw from one another denying the very things that make us human.

"We cannot effectively deal with education, climate change, racial injustice or any other complex issue unless we are grounded in shared responsibility and collective effort." (Sept. 19, 2023, The Christian Citizen, *We are Meant to go Together*)

But, going together requires at a fundamental level, that we see and hear each other and make ourselves seen.

READ BETWEEN MY LEGS

The People on Top – Communicating With Authority

This story is well known by now in my small town of Sonoma, California. There's nothing as funny as the truth. So, this true tale will make you giggle. It's about our medical es-

We are electrical currents. We generate goodwill by extending ourselves.

tablishment, one of many systems that is sagging underneath our need for better communications. My friends call this "The Vagina Story." When I was about 21, I needed a doctor's exam in order to get into college. In those days they required a doctor's visit to prove I was healthy enough to

attend the University. So, I went for my checkup to an older male physician who seemed competent. He looked tired and hunched over, wrinkled and serious.

So, there I was in one of those awful white outfits they give you that open up in the front or the back (I can't remember which it is.) At the miserable moment when I had to spread my legs to let those archaic, cold forceps they used to use to look up my *you know what*, he grimaced. His tiny wire rimmed eyeglasses, like little slits, slipped to the bottom of his nose.

I gasped, now more tense than before after feeling pinched "down there." He looked up at me, his eyes squinting, peeking over the sheet and my knees, with a solemn stare. Then came his words, "You will not EVER be able to have sexual intercourse without major surgery. You have a double hymen."

I was a virgin and this terrified me. I ran home to my mom who was a stubborn woman, smart and strong. There she was – with beady eyes, wearing those tiny eyeglasses, just like his, staring at me from over her newspaper.

I sobbed, "Oh my God, mom – the doctor says I need a serious operation because my vagina is closed up." I screeched, scared of hospitals anyway, and the thought of that kind of surgery, especially in that fragile spot, panicked me.

Mom was immersed in the daily political news, a bull-headed Irish/Norwegian who had lived through a lot.

She curled her upper lip, scoffing, while I was hoping for some sympathy . . . all she uttered were four little words, "get yourself a sailor."

Knowing my mother was a force of nature, I dashed right to the phone. Breathlessly, embarrassed but taking a big gulp of air, I called my friend Joe who was on leave from his navy ship. (A gullible kid . . . I took mom's advice literally.)

Joe actually wore a navy uniform in those days, iron-ically as white as the doctor's outfit. He gleamed with a big Italian smile and a bright, sunny, clean, navy outfit on, one of those stiff hats they wore. He stood taller then, beaming with pride and looking more grown up – having graduated from high school. He was one of those genuine, sweet guys with big, warm, wide brown, doe-eyes. The kind of boy you immediately trusted. I told him the truth, "Joe, can you help me out?"

That was the end of my need for surgery.

THE BLENDER DRINK

Talking to Each Other Can Cure Us

Without community conversations we close down or get stuck (*in more ways than one*) and lose important information. Here's another true story that proves the point with impact:

I was constipated for weeks. Seriously, I couldn't go to the bathroom for a loooong time. Chewing Metamucil cookies and taking stool softeners did no good. I was impacted, for sure.

Poking, prodding, probiotics, primal gut restore tablets, exams or whatever latest laxative was out there – were useless. That forbidden black hole, the rectum of no return was either stopped up or going suddenly.

I took everything the doctors or the Internet told me to – from magnesium citrate to "Go Lightly," a huge gallon of liquid that I now call, "the Wings of Death." That gigantic container was the idea of the young, good looking doctor in the emergency hospital who managed to ignore me for six hours before he suggested it. Luckily, I called my girlfriend, a retired nurse who said, "Oh my God, don't take that!"

Her information helped. But, the other things were

already taking a toll. The citrate drink, in the meantime, was like drinking Clorox. I'd be out on a walk in nature and all of a sudden I'd have to run to the hills. SHE was the one who correctly diagnosed me – I had a form of IBS.

I can't imagine what that bottle of *whatever it was* would have done to me. What's up with doctors these days? Too busy, understaffed, retiring, too young to know enough – he seemed so dis-engaged. Maybe he forgot about me? I finally waddled over in my white shirt with the back open, showing my sore butt, still in my bedroom slippers, asking him if I should go home now. Oh, he stuttered, "sure, just take this." So, I towed the gigantic container home and stuck it in my shed.

Back in bed, after hours of tests and sitting, I still had terrible cramping. I was scared. Could this be a serious cancer? I went to another doctor who gave me more suggestions. The last one said more water and milk of magnesium. My girlfriend said, "no, don't take that either." I ate so many vegetables I looked like a ripe, rotund Santa Claus, but not jolly.

My friend Sylvia texted me. "Got time for a hairball?" It's our way of saying, "want to vent or get out whatever's on your mind?" *She had no idea how ready I was. I definitely had major, impacted hairballs.* Something was stopping me up! What was going on? I wondered all along if this problem was really just stuffed, emotions, fully packed.

With Sylvia on the phone, I let it all out, forgive the pun, going on and on – not in the way I would have preferred. I did wonder how much was me holding in emotional "stuff." I complained so loud I imagined the neighbors could hear me for blocks – about everything from politics to the pandemic

– pondered every solution that might help me get unstuck! She commented calmly, "When I get like that, I just take my blender drink."

"Oh, please!" I thought. After all I've been through, this can't work. Nothing has, but what did I have to lose? (There sure seem to be a lot of puns that go along with this story.) Anyway, she explained an idea she had figured out by reading different things. It worked for her: "It's a full blender of water with a couple of handfuls of celery, about three or so table-spoons of flax seed, and some cilantro."

Two days later I was fine. I was back in the flow again! It's still my "go to" solution.

My point in telling this story is that we need each other, more than we know. Doctors, priests or Presidents just aren't enough to keep us afloat, so to speak. Of course, sometimes we do need real medical help. But, at other times a good chat with a friend or neighbor can be the cure for many problems. Emotional hairballs restore us in more ways than one.

Radical reaching out saved the day. One doctor, one director, one leader – is not enough. If I hadn't learned about the drink from Sylvia, I would probably be taking stool softeners right now or using a plunger.

As George Monbiot makes clear in the *British Guardian:* "If social rupture is not treated as seriously as broken limbs, it's because we cannot see it . . . social pain and physical pain are processed by the same neural circuits . . . This might explain why, in any languages, it is hard to describe the impact of breaking social bonds . . ." (2016) And I was literally impacted.

Now, can we learn to get along?

THE FATHER WOUND

How Men Hurt or Help Us

We crave authority, someone taller, stronger, smarter who must know how to make our lives better. Our inborn belief is that Dad, the one who was supposed to protect us as children, will save us. This longing comes in many forms, whether some kind of King, Emperor, gladiator, etc. Raine Eisler and Douglas Fry, in *Nurturing Our Humanity*, describe it: ". . . our cultural heritage from more domination-oriented times continues to communicate the message that hierarchies of domination are normal, desirable, and inevitable. And this normalization of domination starts very early in life." They add: "and when people experience life in a domination system they tend not to see that there exist more equitable and compassionate, and less stressful and damaging life options."

This study about civilization's challenges was becoming a heavy weight on me. I bet you can relate, I mean, going into the reasons we repeat horrors and damage to civilization isn't exactly light material. So, I decided to get out of my desk chair. I called a guy friend, half-crippled from fingers curled around the keys of my computer, eyes bugging out of my head from staring at the screen, half-blinding me. "Hey, how about a rustic bar stool and some emotional hairballs? I'm just *spent* from working all the time."

So, there we sat at Steiner's, just wanting to relax and find affordable wine. As we chatted the same topic arrived that seems to always circle around conversations a lot these days: why would so many people still promote the mega right, the masked bandit, antagonist, the big guy in the sky?

I had just finished a day of heavy lifting on the topic of patriarchy and a deep emotional day in my psychotherapy practice. My friend opened the chat, "Hey, why in hell do so many people like dictator types?" I murmured one word, "Dad." (We learn from our dads.) My friend looked at me a bit bewildered and then nodded, as if he understood.

As his beer sat waiting, he agreed, ranting about how his father had been tough on him and his self-esteem by being overbearing. His eyes welled up. He seemed to be reliving how his father had never paid attention to him, insisting that he be different, more accomplished, just like "him."

I fell into memory about how I would try to get my dad's attention. I'd stop into his barber shop on the University of Washington Campus in my college years. Excitedly, I'd ask him, how about coffee or lunch? Dad was always too busy. Then, later running through the cafeteria I would sometimes spot him having coffee, reading the newspaper, alone.

Now both of us were in tears, uninvited. Having planned to expand on my usual Irish jokes that night, "I really didn't want to come out tonight to cry at a bar." I was a puddle, twirling my bar stool around in another direction to dry my face.

After wiping my face with my sweater, I spun back around, looking up to all the walls full of big screen TV's. All of them were full of men playing sports or male actors. I pointed to them, saying, "It's everywhere – our heroes."

That took my friend from tears to rally around the topic of the military budgets and football head injuries . . . all the young men trying to find their fathers' approval. And me, longing for it.

But Dad was always at arm's length. The imprint in us says, "Dad . . ." the big man on the screen, the guy on top, the one hovering over us . . . and maybe the one just slightly out of reach, above us.

There is a void, a black hole in our world, where real men might have been . . . men who reveal what's underneath their armor. Brian Klaas has said that we are drawn to the strong man due to evolution and an early anthropological need. It's time to evaluate our choices. (*Corruptible* / Klaas)

We are without models for mature masculinity. There is a dearth of great information about male emotions. There are well-known authors and speakers on the topic – but not a lot of podcasts, films or visuals showing males exhibiting real feelings. Psychotherapist Terrence Real, in *I Don't Want to Talk about It*, writes: "To the degree to which a man learns to be strong, and to devalue weakness, his compassion towards frailty, not just in himself but also in those around him may be limited or condescending . . . the

"I need to hear it, need to sense it, need to know that I am loved. Open your mouth for once, Dad."

– Konrad Stettbacher

loss of expressivity and the loss of vulnerability inevitably lead to diminished connection with others . . ."

Inevitably my clients speak of their dads, usually in denial, believing he was good – no matter what. Sometimes they admit, his imperfections or even neglect – and that brings unbearable grief. We want our dads.

I remember my own father telling me how he grew up and learned to be a man. He said his own father dropped a heavy pitchfork on him as a kid, from a high beam in their barn. Instead of being horrified, his dad acted like he didn't care that he'd nearly killed his young boy – my dear, kind dad was still mad.

Males were taught to wield the sword, instead of dealing with their unmet needs and vulnerabilities

I'll never forget my father's steely glare staring into the distance telling this story. His teeth tightly gripping his cigar, always such a gentle mouth, now he sneered, "I won't ever forget that day." Slowly removing his cigar, his lips sealed shut. As if grunting at his father's grave, his eyes squinted, stony cold. I'd never seen my father like that, and he never mentioned his dad again.

I imagine he wanted to be finished with it. He probably believed he was never loved. I wondered, if his father had embraced him or said anything caring, ever, maybe his life would have been different.

In *Making Sense of Suffering*, Konrad Stettbacher writes about crushing memories and unmet needs that leave us still wanting: "*I need to hear it, need to sense it, need to know that I am loved. Open your mouth for once, Dad."* For most of history, men weren't allowed to have emotions. So, my father buried his dad inside himself and walked away. Sometimes the past stays stuck in us, like a scar. My dear dad was like many in his generation – guys conditioned to be silent, tough or aloof, dominating, rude, and not available. I see their regret and confusion, in my therapy office, underneath the armor. It's not that therapy intends to make parents wrong for being imperfect. But, until we recognize where our patterns originated, we're stuck in old behaviors. Understanding where the pieces fit into the puzzle of psyche helps us heal.

Males were taught to wield the sword, instead of dealing with their unmet needs and vulnerabilities. They suffer from it. In the western world, males are four times more likely to die of suicide than women, more likely to use illicit drugs, endure alcohol related hospitalizations and death. "Subjects who reported receiving higher levels of childhood punishment were significantly more angry than low-punishment subjects. Their anger also predicted the punitiveness of their political attitudes, with subjects expressing higher levels of anger holding more conservative political opinions." (Research from Levine 1996 in *Raised to Rage*, Milburn and Conrad.) So, the beat goes on and legacies continue.

Will young men growing up next give their children a model for an integrated male, capable of assertion, kindness, emotion and intimacy? We learn from our families as Galit Atlas wrote, "Our family colluded and shared the unspoken understanding that silence was the best way to erase what was unpleasant. The assumption in those days that what you don't remember won't hurt you." (Galit Atlas, Ph.D., *Emotional Inheritance*.) I believe the evolution of our species is grinding slowly forward if only we each do one thing differently every-day . . . talk and listen.

I'm deeply moved by my client's work. I tell them often, "You're doing work for the world. Your children and the next generation will know how to communicate through conflict." Barriers and walls, national or personal defenses block belonging. They manifest in stern words, sore backs, passivity or a secretly crumbling Humpty Dumpty with a nice guy front. But, the world needs something else desperately, as Terrence Real writes: "*Sons don't want their father's balls; they want their hearts.*"

> "*Sons don't want their father's balls; they want their hearts.*"
>
> – Terrence Real

Flooded feelings can trigger males to implode or get depressed. Having permission for only anger and none of the other emotions can cause a multitude of consequences including heart attacks, addictions, illness, repressed experiences of gratitude and love, memory, etc.

Let's ponder great men.

I still yearn, long after his passing, to walk beside my dad to the coffee shop.

FROM CHAOS TO UNIFICATION

Speaking Up or Not?

I listened to a mother and her daughter in a therapy session this week. Their anger erupted at a breathtaking pace. The dizzying speed of raging words made me hold onto my seat. Their mutual fears, their anguish and anxiety about abandonment raised the roof. Then they lowered into pain, each admitting the part they played in their splitting apart. Decades of learned family behaviors were being re-enacted. Four days after the session I was still gripped with grief – my own transference. I wondered, how would my life had been better if I had done therapy with my parents? What still lurks in our closets, poisoning our lives?

Anne Lamott chronicles our lives, our cultural and personal challenges, crisply and with whimsy: "Each day the data stream is even more bizarre and disheartening . . . you steadfastly love and serve everyone, see people through tribulation, savor the relief, and give thanks, then, boing – a new setback. It's like tucking an octopus into bed at night: new arms keep popping out." (*Dusk, Night, Dawn: On Revival and Courage*)

As David Bohm, renowned physicist and theorist, wrote, "It has become urgent that we communicate. We have to share our consciousness and to be able to think together, in order to do intelligently whatever is necessary." (David Bohm, *On Dialogue*)

Our power of speech has been constantly threatened. Even our journalists are being jailed or be-headed all over the world. Newspapers and alternative news and great interviewers, once a commodity, are disappearing. The United States has lost some 37,000 newsroom jobs since 2016. (Axios, June 2021). Media is pressured by corporate money to speak sideways, much more about general information or false facts and sometimes not even knowing the truth.

"The most common way people give up their power is by thinking they don't have any."

– Alice Walker

If we are going to exchange words, we also need to notice if they say something or are hollow. These days we "codify," . . . rules. What does that mean? We "cull" wild horses or bison. This language removes us further from each other and empathy . . . culling is killing, murder, violence, hurting, maiming. These words are stale. We call senseless slaughter "genocide" so that nobody feels.

Author Alice Walker (*The Color Purple*) said: "The most common way people give up their power is by thinking they don't have any." We have the power of our voices if we learn to use them. I am heartened by many pioneers working toward a new collective of people teaching conflict skills. Peter

Coleman's work and so many others have given me hope. He talks about how there are now between "7,000 and 10,000 groups" doing various kinds of mediation in different parts of the United States to bridge divides.

We have herculean work to do, but brave people, called to the task are stepping up. The Truth and Reconciliation groups help with hearing stories of abuse and damage, from Indian cultures to South African. Global endeavors bring respectful dialogue to humanity, wanting to learn how to do it. (Bridging Divides Initiative, Princeton/ Ted Talk/ 3/16/22 Coleman, *The Way Out*)

Our urgency to communicate better is being recognized. Medical people need to talk to each other. The ear doctor could speak to the eye doctor, eventually offering more quality of care in our medical systems everywhere. Workers want to be heard by employers and organizations need to be reachable so that we can be heard, etc. Available counseling and mediation services are essential and need to be affordable.

While we seem hell bent on this eve of destruction, to keep repeating our past horrors, I see wondrous repair emerging between people, in my therapy practice. I read about many endeavors to forage a civil way to live.

HOUSING HAIRBALL

Giving Away our Power and Money

I learned about the power of moving from conflict to communication the hard way many times. This was one of them. In 2008 and 2009 I lived in foreclosure hell. Dozens of black printed letters at the door, sleeplessness, auction dates, signs on the door, and strange men taking photos of the house, with no warning – this became my life. The bank "reviewed my file" for almost two years. Was it in the lost and found?

People have asked me to write about it but I didn't want to. It's unbearably painful and, honestly, I doubted anyone would believe the ending. But, I realize, it has to be told because it's about persistence and having a voice. In one second we can lose our power.

We've all read about foreclosures, but when someone wants to take your home of twenty-five years, your guts crunch, your heart palpitates late into the night. It's like having someone stand over you with an ax, threatening to sever your limbs. The anguish has few words to match it. But, I have to try.

In 2009 I phoned my bank. "I've paid my mortgage for 25 years but I'm going through job loss and a divorce.

Can you help?" Chase replied, "The only way we can modify your loan is if you quit paying." After repeated calls to bank representatives who verified the same thing, I quit paying. I'd never heard of a bank lying.

I spent the next two years chasing down Chase to get my own home back. I was constantly rushing to the bank with documents, faxing information and filling out forms. Meanwhile, I got big black foreclosure letters tacked to my front door, with a loud thump, while voicemails continued from them every day. Relentless abuse.

At night I had panic attacks and took more tranquilizers than I can name. What did I do wrong to make this happen to me?

Every week a new "rep" was in charge of my file. I didn't know where all my bank statements and docs landed, on which desk in which office with which clerk. Every week the papers I sent disappeared, as if sucked into some vortex. The documents were lost or the bank needed new ones, the clerk who promised to be "my representative" could no longer be reached, no one knew why. They said they had no idea what happened to him. Were people jumping ship, getting fired, what?

On a typical day, I was told with vehemence, "you now have a committed, portfolio manager." Then the new person needed 60 more pages faxed to them because the computer "couldn't transfer my documents from the day before." Two "loan mod" companies I paid to help me took my cash, saying it would cost less to pay that way. Then they disappeared, gone – their phones, faxes, and physical offices tacked shut. I had meetings with them sometimes in person, on just the previous day – in that same office. Twenty-four hours later, it was boarded up. I tried every phone number and contact I had – gone, gone, gone.

One cold morning a neighbor stopped by when I was getting my mail. I pulled out eighteen letters from the bank in the box. I waved them in the air, "can you believe the number of trees that were cut to make all these?" Someone walked by sighing, "I see the house is being auctioned in the newspaper, next Saturday." I asked in disbelief, "When?" The feeling is hard to capture. It was nothing I ever thought could happen in my life; it was like something out of a horror movie.

At night I had panic attacks and took more tranquilizers than I can name. If I lost the house where could I go? Would I live in my car? I looked at rentals but most would not take two dogs. What did I do wrong to make this happen to me? In all of my history, I had only seen banks do what they planned. My parents owned and sold a few humble homes before they died. I had never heard of anything like this.

The hardest memory was on Christmas Eve. I pleaded with the seemingly polite Chase representative, "Christmas day is my birthday. I so much need tomorrow off. Are we complete for now?" The guy responded so sweetly, "You are fine. Just relax for the holidays." I appealed again, "Are you sure?" Oh, he sounded sincere; he was absolutely positive. On Christmas day there were more big black notices loudly pounded to my door. I was in complete disbelief. Christmas day even?

For years I paid my mortgage on time, planting trees and lilacs, and the like – home meant comfort, eating bagels, pajamas, cats and dogs sniffing the backyard bushes. Trauma took their place. In extreme shock, I felt psychically dismembered in a moral, mental and financial way.

What was my part in this? I was naive, trusting them when I should have been more awake. *I gave away my power.* I dis-associated from myself. Geneen Roth writes about her own losses with Madoff's stock stealing, in *Lost and Found*: "despite having lost thirty years of savings, I still wasn't sure how we would live or where. And it was clear that the teeny issue of my relationship with money – examining my beliefs and behavior felt like riding a Ferris wheel."

Yes, I had to admit it, take an itsy, bitsy bit of responsibility – I did refinance too much. I used the money to get my master's degree, become a therapist, write a book and host radio. I hadn't planned finances well enough. I ran off into a romantic relationship hoping he would rescue me. I was a victim to my own romanticism, my reluctance to face practicality. But, getting insight should not be polluted with self-criticism. Beating myself up was more abuse. Belaboring our mistakes doesn't heal anything either. Geneen Roth adds: "After Madoff's confession, living in the mind was like trying to run on broken glass. I'd wake up in the middle of the night in terror. I desperately wanted to turn back the clock. I wanted to know then what I know now."

So, I finally hired a woman who was losing her house too, but good with numbers. Sometimes we have to borrow strength from others or a character trait we are growing. She was mathematical. She knew how to check off those God awful boxes. Becky was a bit of a bully, brutish and mean sometimes, but she got the job done. Every week she'd blurt, "there's no way in hell you are ever getting this house back. If you ever do, we'll crack champagne, but there's no way."

There were two moments in time I will never forget. My first husband, Richard Byrne, called to see how I was doing. I was weak and worn. He asked what I wanted to pay them every month. I told him. Then he asked me this ballsy question, *"why don't you call and tell them what you want?"* I was aghast. Me? Little old me ask a great big bank for what I want? Are you kidding? I bellowed, "YOU WANT ME TO TELL THE BANK WHAT I NEED?"

I was in crisis. As Bessel van der Kolk wrote so rightly, "The essence of psychological trauma is a loss of faith that there is order and continuity in life . . . . Trauma occurs when one loses the sense of having a safe place to retreat to – within or outside of oneself – to deal with frightening emotions or experiences. This results in a state of helplessness . . . . a feeling that one's actions have no bearing on the outcome of ones' life . . . " (*The Body Keeps the Score*).

Well, what the hell? If ever I had done radical reaching out, it was for those two gruesome years. I telephoned my "portfolio" representative, Brian Rutherford. Finally, an "advocate" as they began to call them, actually stayed with me for two full months. Though I couldn't reach him half the time, I did get him that day. *I told him what I wanted.*

Finding my voice in this chaos was a steep climb. I knew about persistence and grit, so I called and wrote him letters almost every day. I told the truth, using my "I" statements. I wrote him about my lack of family to relocate with, my freezing cold house, my two dogs shivering. I shared the way my parents died leaving me just enough money to buy my home. I wrote about how I had the intention of being responsible all my life. I told him I was scared to death.

On that last day, I called again, "had they reviewed my portfolio yet? Was the house the banks or mine?" Hard to believe an institution can just yank a home from under a person, like a carpet. I had just done what they suggested, "Stop paying your mortgage for a few weeks – then we'll help you refinance." (That was their rote response to millions of people.) He said, "Oh my supervisor was going to review those and make a decision this week, hold on, let me give her a call." I sat, the way I had sat waiting, for those two years.

The house seemed hollow, as if full of "ghosts," my eyes like "empty sockets . . ." sometime songs come to me when words disappear. The Paul Simon song, *Graceland*, passed through my mind. When he came back to the phone there was a long pause. Oh how tired I was of long pauses. He had talked to her. I gasped, "what did she say?" Another pause. Was he still on the other end of the line? Was he distracted by her call? Had she gotten upset with the paperwork not done correctly?

What? "What did she say?" I begged. He said words I always have trouble telling anyone, because I don't think they will believe me. "She said, 'tell Katy I love her.'"

I had never met this woman. I didn't even know her name. (And I could never track either of them down again when it was all over.) All I could imagine was that she had read my letters full of self-disclosure and raw honesty – it's all I had. "Please give me my house back. I am a good person. I help people in my counseling work, my parents are gone, my dogs need housing. I thought the bank said I had to quit paying in order to re-finance."

The next day I got the certified letter with their loan modification agreement. I ran to three mathematically minded friends to look over the docs. One said, "I just can't believe this. It is an incredible loan." They gave me the exact price I requested that day when I told them what I wanted to pay.

I called the woman that had been tough on me, but also helped me a hell of a lot. "Hi Becky," it was my turn to pause. "Well, I have news." She asked, "Did you hear from the bank?" Then came my turn to pause, then my three little words: "crack the champagne."

Perseverance, moral outrage, constant communication, asking for help from community and radical reaching out. It took all of that, prayers and activists in my village to lean on too.

Change takes balls, not just friends listening to our emotional hairballs. It demands insistence on dignity and courage that calls on us from the groin. Transformation and changing a system requires all of our involvement, individually and in relationships. Real power means audacious authenticity and not allowing ourselves to be prisoners of our own fears.

Eight million homes were lost during the foreclosure crisis of '08 – '09. The personal is political. The middle and lower classes are losing the ability to find food and housing. This makes maturing impossible. My understanding of the great Abraham Maslow, American Psychologist is that his steps to fulfillment are: Food, shelter, to love and be loved and then self-actualization. Humanity is bolstered by basic physical needs for safety and security in order to self-actualize. The rise of this new greedy corporate class of homeowners is grotesque, criminal, cruel – it slashes and cuts away at our ability to grow beyond fear. "Back in the 90's well over 90% of homes were owned by people. This is no longer the case." (1/23/2020 Glantz/Kera news by Courtney Collins.) We need our homes. It's macabre in the town I live in, houses are being bought out by wealth. It's become a monopoly game. Many of them sit empty because their "owners" are on Caribbean cruises, while the rest grovel at two jobs, trying to pay impossibly high rents.

The economy matters. It's a part of feeling safe. How is it that some man at the top of a hill makes all our decisions along with a bunch of other guys and a few lucky women? Marion Wright Edelman, president of the Children's Defense Fund, said, "A child dies from guns every ninety-eight minutes in this country, and from poverty every fifty-three minutes, and from child abuse every seven hours." She expanded, "They're proposing to cut two hundred and fifty billion dollars from programs for poor children, poor families, disabled children – and it's not even to balance the budget!" (Interview with Calvin Thompkins, 1996)

What lessons have we learned from having money or being without it? The truth that's starting to come out is that wealthy people are also stressed. "New studies show that status and wealth gaps make everyone – including the rich and powerful – more anxious and insecure . . . another adverse effect of hierarchies of domination seems to be that the people on top tend to be psychologically disconnected from those around them . . . The large gap between the haves and have nots that characterizes domination systems is itself highly stressful." (Riane Eisler and Douglas P. Fry, *Nurturing Our Humanity*)

What to do? We need to stay engaged in conversations everywhere. Communication and asking for what we want – *these are our walking sticks*. We can design a new paradigm, re-arrange these monolithic forces. We, the people, can do it.

Brian Klaas, in his studies, asks why we continually end up with power-hungry, narcissistic leaders. Why do we keep getting bludgeoned by big corporations and boisterous leaders? *Are we to blame?* Why are we drawn to people who want to abuse us? Conquer and dominate rather than serve. Psychopaths are heads of countries or organizations. They're drawn to it from anthropological instinct. Prehistoric

History and generations of trauma are embodied in us

societies needed physical prowess and strength. We still have that template in our brains. He suggests that we design systems to evaluate these people. (Klaas, *Big Think*, 02/19/2023.) It's time we rethink who runs our world. *You can't have democracy without mental health.*

We could have *momentum if we moved through our own divides and worked together*. It took a village to keep me propped up. *We, the people need power within and between ourselves, not power over us.* Imagine. More homes for us all, food, jobs, healthcare, climate calming, safety.

As Theodore Roethke wrote: "What we need is more people that specialize in the impossible." I would add, what we need is more people talking to each other.

CHANGE AND GETTING TO THE BOTTOM OF IT

My Addiction / Overeating Days

What makes change happen? Conversations with ourselves are just as important as those between us. As Galit Atlas Ph.D writes: "The secrets we keep from ourselves are meant to protect us [from] the realities that are too threatening to know or that we can't fully process."

I want to disclose a divide that existed inside my own psyche. My story might be a less severe example of how evil co-exists in us or how the Nazi's slaughtered six million Jews. Fortunately for me, mine was not murderous – but in a way it was slowly killing me.

Most of us carry parts . . . maybe one of them wants to stay home from work and the other is ambitious, or one part wants to look at pornography and another part wants to be a good religious boy, etc. Or one part drinks too much Vodka, while the other part wants radiant health. Any compulsion begs us to unbury it, to reconcile our inner selves.

I remember when I couldn't stop eating. I lugged bags of food to my apartment and ate until I was in pain. I devoured doughnuts, pizza, whatever I could find. At 300 pounds, I hid at the back table in restaurants, dodging leering eyes.

I was in complete despair and full of self-loathing. The worst part was I couldn't figure out what was going on. Why didn't I have more discipline? Why couldn't I stay on a diet? Was my body not processing food properly? Did I have allergies? Did I have thyroid problems? Was I a major depressive? What?

After ten years of therapy, dieting, fasting, meditating in India, twelve step programs, medical tests, and studying nutrition, I was giving up. Then, something unpredictable happened. In one therapy session my eating habits changed.

> *If we haven't been loved well, recognized, understood . . . we lower our expectations.*
> *We stop asking for what we need.*
> *We stop showing the places that hurt or need comfort.*
>
> – Geneen Roth

Counseling my clients is one thing. Being in therapy myself is another. Both are brave. My therapist asked me what was going on in my gut. Unforeseen sobs came from somewhere new to me. The cries were guttural. She put her hand on my stomach. Howling came out of me, like someone trapped in a dungeon. Then came the words: "I'm lonely. I don't feel loved." I imagined this voice came from a long forgotten small child holding out her hands for me.

That night, as I stared into the open fridge, my evening ritual – I forced myself to try something different. I knew after hearing that bottomless sobbing in my counseling session, I had to understand that echoing, wailing sound.

"I just want to talk to you," I muttered, feeling agitated and awkward talking to myself at the open fridge. I didn't even believe in the latest new age books about the "inner child." I was disgusted with my own struggle, now this silly talking to myself was a part of the horror show.

Without any patience for the entire ordeal, I wanted to make this quick and get on with my eating. I pondered plastic surgery – there had to be another way out. I pretended this so-called inner kid was standing beside me. I stood there, at the slightly open refrigerator door, with cold air creeping out, in the middle of winter, glaring into the fridge. I whispered, "You can have anything you want. Can we just talk for a minute?"

She seemed to be inside me somewhere, because I felt her ravenous and rebellious ravings. "I want pizza! I want it! Give it to me!"

History and generations of trauma are embodied in us. Sure, I thought, for a split second, "This is the stupidest thing I've ever done. I'm just going to eat the pizza. Fuck it." Thank God nobody could see me. Was I crazy? Maybe I was making up some kind of theatre. But, the voice that came out of me that day in therapy hissed like a hungry stray animal, or a gnarly ancient jungle creature, lost in the forest. I knew it meant something.

So, I said, "Okay, okay. You can have pizza. But, are you sure that's what you want? Because I promise you can have anything you really want."

I knew from having read Geneen Roth's book, *When*

Food is Love, at least intellectually, that inside a food obsessed person there is deprivation. We never feel deserving of what we need and that includes eating what we really want. She writes: ". . . if we haven't been loved well, recognized, understood . . . we lower our expectations. We stop asking for what we need. We stop showing the places that hurt or need comfort. We stop expecting to be met and we begin to rely on ourselves, and only ourselves to provide sustenance, comfort and pleasure. We begin to eat. And eat."

I had read about how people with food problems hungered for a loving mother. In that few seconds, in the icy air at the refrigerator, I found another part, a kind person inside me. She asked, "What do you really need?"

Then there was a pause that lasted forever, "I don't know . . . no one has ever asked before. "I really just want my flannel pajamas and a bath." She was shy, "I just want hot milk and crackers and my teddy bear."

That was the 60 seconds that changed my life.

I fixed her hot milk. I literally gave myself soda crackers and a warm bath. Desperation does odd things to behavior. But, I swear to God, I imagined us both going to bed that night in flannel pajamas, holding a teddy bear. That was the first night I remember not overeating. I heard her, finally and found an inner "good mother."

During those early years I carried out agonizing, unconscious rituals with food: hiding, hoarding, craving, planning, restless for ice cream, chips or candy bars, stocking them in freezers, closets and cupboards, I never felt lovable. That famished part of me was what I knew.

People think addicts lack discipline. But, for many of us, the root of obsessive overeating, starving ourselves, controlling our food or substances is not laziness. This includes infinite compulsions: being tethered to your phone, sex obsession, anorexia and alcohol, etc. We want to feel worthy of our wants and real hungers.

I couldn't even answer my therapist when she asked me what I really needed. I believed that having what I wanted was impossible.

Weeks and months went by. I started living my life differently. I remember one afternoon that was a turning point. I stopped at one of my very favorite bakeries on North Beach, San Francisco. Stella's! It's famous for a huge glass case, full of a wonderland of eclairs, custard covered buns and layered pieces of luscious cakes to die for. Every surface in the place is bursting with scrumptious, mouth-watering, fancy buns and rolls, with whiffs of sweet smelling, marshmallow whipped cream. I stood in front of that counter, telling "my kid" she could have ANYTHING she wanted. That day she said she wasn't hungry. I will never forget it! I had never felt like that. When I was finally free from guilt and being beat up by the mean inner voice, it was kind of weird how easy it was.

I'm sick and tired of the pressure to be thin.

It's time that women feel good about being big.

As Geneen Roth writes: I began "undoing twenty years of brainwashing. Of being told my hungers are bottomless and that I must be vigilant in my attempt at controlling them. I am not spineless. I am not devouring. I do not need to be afraid of myself.

I can and I will trust myself to embrace what is life-giving and to dismiss what will destroy me. I am lovable. I am loving. My choices about food will reflect that if I give myself a chance."

Though I made a choice to eat differently, another divide inside me was political anger. We are "fed" stories about how we "should be" that hurt us. I was outraged at society's pressure to be thin. Queen Latifah has begun a new endeavor: no more "plus sizes," starting a new movement: "It's Bigger Than Me" campaign . . . to change the conversation surrounding obesity (Oct 8, Cathy Cassata, 2021.) "That obesity is a manageable health condition, not a character flaw," she highlights the stigma, self-hate, and shame felt in our society around this condition . . . another way that being different is chastised.

> *"Fat isn't the problem.*
>
> *Dieting is the problem.*
>
> *A society that rejects anyone*
>
> *whose body shape or size doesn't*
>
> *match an impossible ideal*
>
> *is the problem.*
>
> *A medical establishment that*
>
> *equates 'thin' with 'healthy'*
>
> *is the problem."*
>
> – Linda Bacon

I admit, I'm sick and tired of the pressure to be thin. It's time that women feel good about being big. I mean, big, big, big in every possible way. We are half the world and our full power and permission to be all of ourselves has come. Times up on prejudices against us.

Go ahead and eat girls; you need the fuel.

And men need freedom too – freedom from pressures perhaps unknown to you but burdensome, stealing your life force, like always being strong and emotionless.

I've found a few really inspiring women, among them, of all things, Linda Bacon. Yes, it's really her name. Here's one of her posts: "Fat isn't the problem. Dieting is the problem. A society that rejects anyone whose body shape or size doesn't match an impossible ideal is the problem. A medical establishment that equates 'thin' with 'healthy' is the problem." The solution? *Health at Every Size.*

My male clients suffer too. More men call me now for therapy and marriage counseling than women. They are isolated, trying too hard to impress, to perform, or to be potent. As Terrence Real wrote about men's confusion, "What men have been promised is an appreciative, saintly wife – a whore in the bedroom, a kitten on the living room couch, a scintillating cocktail companion, and a damn fine cook and homemaker. This is not a mature relationship." (*I Don't Want to Talk About It.*) But for females, Roth puts it well in her book, *This Messy Magnificent Life*: "Might this be another way the patriarchy controls women's bodies? By hypnotizing us into believing we must be thin in order to have value, or authority? If I wanted to silence half the population of the world – I can't think of a better way to do it. Expecting a woman to stand up for what she knows while convincing her that she must first be thin is like binding a Chinese woman's feet and asking her to run a marathon."

Unfortunately, women have also applied these standards against each other. We've "eaten" the idea that men or media dictate our weight, that softness is weak. Of course now, even males are getting hit with media's message to be skinny at all costs. As Caroline Dooner so outspokenly writes: "It comes down to wanting to be happy more than you want to be beautiful, because if you feel worthy, even if you believe you aren't quite beautiful, you can't lose." (*The Fuck It Diet: Eating Should be Easy*)

We're indoctrinated. Dominated by patriarchal messages towering over us with pressures to comply to teeny, tiny, smallness. We are told slender is better – that big, robust personalities and bodies take up too much space. I applaud healthiness (big or small), but that also means listening to our gut.

PALPABLE FAITH

Blind faith is not enough. It's toothless over time. In contrast, faith that is in our feet combined with goodness moves mountains. Man's belief in God or spirituality can help us commune in harmony, but it can also lead to religious wars. But, good communication gives us compassion, consensus, and communion. John F. Kennedy said, "Our problems are self-imposed – therefore, they can be solved by us. And humankind can be exactly as we want it to be. No problem of human destiny is beyond human beings. Our reason and spirit have often solved the seemingly unsolvable." (Kennedy's address / American University, Wash D.C. June 10, 1963)

Great minds have captured fathomable faith through the centuries. So, I'll borrow their wisdom while I put words to our human potential, to the unified field and a "quantum leap" for civilization.

Leonard Cohen, singer/songwriter, spent years in a monastery reflecting. He realized through his sorrow, "There is a crack, a crack in everything that's how the light gets in." (Anthem) If we keep peeking through the cracks, we'll create something new. Terry Patten offers: "More than three billion people have Internet access today, and within the next few years five billion will . . . This gives us an extraordinary capacity to communicate." He adds: "our bonds of appropriate mutual trust have been rapidly declining . . . Such a profound cultural shift is a considerable undertaking that must overcome formidable obstacles. But we are hardly impotent. Our individual transformations can synergistically exert disproportionate power – through many avenues, including, as Ken Wilbur pointed out: 'When 10 percent of the population grow into a genuinely higher structure of consciousness, the nature of public agreements and power exchanges can be restructured according to a higher set of rules.'" (*A New Republic of the Heart*, Patten)

Collective courage must come first, wisdom second, and serenity only at the very end.

A shift in consciousness will require momentum, not rest. Palpable faith is not sitting on clouds with angels playing harps, lulling us to slumber. Maybe that's what religion has done too much of – putting us to sleep. Social movements and each of us doing something helpful in our communities is faith in action. I respect meditation as another powerful tool for awareness, but it's not my emphasis here. Real spirituality includes grit work, active concern for our common good, here on earth. *What good is God if we are still killing each other or withdrawing from engagement?*

If we engage in delicate dialogues with the same fervor as we do flying to the moon, paying the Pope or building bombs and bullets, we'll establish trust between us. "Know the truth, and the truth shall make you free." (Bible, John, 8: 31-32)

Richard Hatch wrote: "I experience God whenever I express my truth in the world – and that is when I have the courage to stand up and express the energy that's inside my heart . . . When I hold back any part of myself, I feel just the opposite." (*The Experience of God*)

Someone I admire beyond words explained faith in action: Ady Barkan, a journalist for *The Nation and Political Activist,* on Sept 30, 2016, celebrated an eleven-year marriage with his wife Rachel. Their baby, Carl, a four-month old was just waking up to the wonders of the universe. A week later, at the age of 32, he was given a death sentence. The doctor told him he had ALS – which would destroy all connections between his brain and muscles, leading to complete paralysis and death.

Ady wrote about the serenity prayer before he died on Nov.1, 2023: "God, grant me the serenity to accept the things I cannot change, the courage to change the things I can, and the wisdom to know the difference." He added: "There is a seeming paradox embedded in the third part of Niebuhr's prayer, because the wisdom to know the difference between what we can and cannot change can only be earned through struggle. Neuroscientists seek a cure for ALS *because they do not accept*

"Uncertainty about the reliability and availability of support creates what Bowlby calls 'anxious attachment behaviors' such as clinging, fear of separation, and requests for reassurance, in adults as well as children."
– Silencing the Self,
Dana Jack

134

its inevitability. Organizers rage against the machines of capitalism with that same determination. It is only by refusing to accept the complacency of previous generations that the impossible becomes reality. For me, Niebuhr's prayer is most true if rearranged: Collective courage must come first, wisdom second, and serenity only at the very end." (*The Nation*, 11/5/2018)

The twelve step programs are one of several organizations that have sustained important values over time because they put principles before personalities – before ego. I am not minimizing what they offer, but Barkan's view also matters.

The new hero is us. If we reach toward each other – we have the potential to move from conflict to communication. Even reparations, though helpful – are not enough in the long run. To give an apology and walk away – can be another band aid, a way to try to forget. We need to share our pain, grief, fear, needs, our solutions.

> *"Man did not weave the web of life; he is merely a strand in it. Whatever he does to the web, he does to himself."*
>
> – Chief Seattle

In our criminal justice systems – prisons, government, corporations, everywhere – can we bring our voices? "The wounds of trauma are not merely those caused by the perpetrators of violence and exploitation . . . these wounds are part of the social ecology of violence, in which crimes against subordinated and marginalized people are rationalized, tolerated, or rendered invisible." (Judith L. Herman, MD, *Truth and Repair*.) Humanity's inability to accomplish collaboration is manifesting in loss of intimacy with all life.

So, how can we ensure serenity on this battling planet? We need safe conversations, learning about our own complicated impulses and history. When we own up to and uproot our toxic urges and thoughts, we concretize faith. Cohesion, civility, communication, and circulating arise from crucial conversations – the "c's" of connection. A survey found that when participants sit together with divergent political views, "even a two-hour conversation was enough for them to understand each other's perspective." (*The Lonely Century*, Noreena Hertz)

When we build trustworthy relationships we'll propel palpable faith. As Dana Jack wrote: "Uncertainty about the reliability and availability of support creates what Bowlby calls 'anxious attachment behaviors' such as clinging, fear of separation, and requests for reassurance, in adults as well as children." (*Silencing the Self*)

On a personal plane, while watching clients stuck in gridlock, despairing of repair, when they start exploring their impulses with curiosity – that's how their resentments are removed. They shift from their cover-ups and defenses to empathy – this is the outcome of the power of dialogue. Chief Seattle knew in the 1860's: "Man did not weave the web of life; he is merely a strand in it. Whatever he does to the web, he does to himself." (All things are bound together, all things connect.) Isn't it time we repaired our divorce with ourselves and nature?

African American author, Anthony Hinton, lived through thirty years on death row, wrongfully. I must tell you, I had the honor of meeting him recently. Being in his presence widened me. I was thrust into spaciousness, looking into his face. He writes: "We've got to learn to love one another or else we'll destroy each other." Hinton saw this from the entrails of jail. His penetrating and poignant story tells us to *lean in*. He urges: "we've got to learn to talk to one another." (*The Sun Does Shine*)

When we unify, we transcend. We lighten into luminosity. We touch divinity by loving our neighbor and by moving beyond ego. We have all, in some moment or another, entered the unified field. I always joke about it, saying, "that's why people emote, 'O God,' when they have orgasms."

As Rumi wrote:

"The wound is the place where the light enters you."

At the end of his life, a great genius articulated the unified field. Albert Einstein made his last, final discovery. He wrote to his daughter, Lieserl:

> *When I proposed the theory of relativity, very few understood me, and what I will reveal now to transmit to mankind will also collide with the misunderstanding and prejudice in the world . . . There is an extremely powerful force that, so far, science has not found a formal explanation to. It is a force that includes and governs all others, and is even behind any phenomenon operating in the universe and has not yet been identified by us. This universal force is LOVE. Love is God and God is Love.*
>
> *This is the variable that we have ignored for too long, maybe because we are afraid of love because it is the only energy in the universe that man has not learned to drive at will.*

To give visibility to love, I made a simple substitution in my most famous equation. If instead of E = mc², we accept that the energy to heal the world can be obtained through love multiplied by the speed of light squared, we arrive at the conclusion that love is the most powerful force there is, because it has no limits.

Each individual carries within them a small but powerful generator of love whose energy is waiting to be released. I deeply regret not having been able to express what is in my heart, which has quietly beaten for you all my life. Maybe it's too late to apologize, but as time is relative, I need to tell you that I love you and thanks to you I have reached the ultimate answer!

Your father,
Albert Einstein

(suedreamwalker.wordpress.com, 2015/04/15, a letter from Albert Einstein to his daughter. *Edited from original*)

Just as I was finishing this book, synchronistically, a lost friend of thirty years called. In our former years of conversations, I had often asked him to talk about his emotions and he'd said he wasn't interested in feelings. He was enthralled by meditation and studying philosophy and politics. He wanted to be happy. Approaching eighty, he still wanted to do a guided "trip" on psilocybin. He wanted a breakthrough so that his meditation and sitting practice would become more expansive.

After the trip, he said he'd sobbed uncontrollably for seven hours on the drug. His inner child came out and they talked for those long hours! He said he reassured his inner little boy that he would never forget about him again. Meditation can make us more aware, but can it open gates to major healing?

Was *that* a spiritual journey or a metamorphosis? We have to resurrect what's buried in us. "The wound is the place where the light enters you." – Rumi. We all lug around long learned earthly habits, harboring hatred and self-loathing. Even the psychedelic drug world may aid the brain in reversing our instinct to tether and harm life. If used responsibly perhaps they will also illuminate unity. (I don't take them now or espouse drugs without guidance, just to be clear.) Although, my own trip on mescaline offered a visceral view of unity. I saw a sliced orange with cells breathing. I witnessed trees inhaling and exhaling, veins in my hands pulsating in vivid purple. Used with great caution, this offers another world view.

Don Lattin's book, *God on Psychedelics*, describes his research, having been a religious writer for the SF Chronicle. Michael Pollan, Margaret Meade, and others have attempted to offer information and guides to supply safe places for the exploration of consciousness. Sam Harris explores this realm in *Waking Up:*

"I believe that psychedelics may be indispensable for some people – especially those who, like me, initially need convincing that profound changes in consciousness are possible." He adds, "I can say that the true goal of meditation is more profound than most people realize . . . It is quite possible to lose one's sense of being a separate self and to experience a kind of boundless, open awareness – to feel in other words, at one with the cosmos."

However you get to the core of yourself, you find a more primeval yearning to care and connect. I call this "going down the ladder."

There are many approaches to creating cohesion and expanding our awareness into more unity and joy. Insoo Kim Berg, a Korean born psychotherapist, once demonstrated the power of wishes. Videos of her client sessions were enthralling. When she asked them what they wished for, their depression or anxiety faded – their postures changed, they sat up taller, their faces lit up. We humans thrive with safety and support.

Still, evil lurks. Bruce Perry, trauma researcher has studied peoples negative, cruel, heinous impulses: "The desire to stay in the in-group will cause some of us to follow a bully and do things we'd never have done on our own . . ." He explains how reflexively we can join destructive groups: "Fear shuts down the reasoning and reflective part of our brain . . . We're also more compliant toward authority." (*The Long Shadow*/ Jeanne Supin/ The Sun Magazine/Nov 2016)

But, repairing our inner divides is possible. The power of dialogue is profound. I can actually view, in my counseling sessions, people breaking through their confusion or gridlock. A translucent energy appears, numinosity, when they feel understood.

In the beginning was the Word. If God is love, I doubt that God would want us causing suffering. There are no winners on a dead earth.

The evolution of the species will require us all becoming conscious through conversations, counseling and teaching. As Milburn and Conrad reiterate in *Raised to Rage*: kids need to "learn history. They need systematic and thorough training in such skills as conflict resolution, negotiation, management of emotions and child rearing . . . because so many young children see violence in their everyday life – in their families or in their neighborhoods – schools also need to institute programs to heal children who have been exposed to violence."

So, we stand in front of overwhelming threats to safety today. *Harnessing our unkind impulses, is our next step.* Terry Patten summarizes our overwhelming, complex crisis and potential, "Never have we faced such serious and likely lasting changes in the planetary biosphere. Only recently have we become able to even conceive of such events . . . Our entire way of being with ourselves and one another-individually, mutually, and collectively – is now under evolutionary pressure to manifest radical new emergent properties. This, I believe, creates the conditions for tremendous potential and hope." (*A New Republic of the Heart*)

We can all participate. As David Brooks wrote, "The people who radiated a permanent joy have given themselves over to lives of deep and loving commitment. Giving has become their nature, and little by little they have made their souls incandescent." (*The Second Mountains*)

Reverberating reverence and awe arrives from deep disclosure, dialogue, and community connection. When we understand our own wounds and each other's, we become humble warriors. As Rumi wrote, "Out beyond ideas of wrongdoing and rightdoing, there's a field. I'll meet you there."

CONCLUSION

Finding Closure

This chapter is called "Closure." But beware, I don't believe in complete closure. Pauline Boss, Ph.D. explains it in her book *Ambiguous Loss*. Instead of closure she calls endings "continuing bonds."

In our world today we want tidy answers, which in part has contributed to our impatience with process and cutting off our curiosity and empathy. But, our ability to grieve and stay in communication is the key to freedom and liberty for all. As Francis Weller wrote, "The work of a mature person is to carry grief in one hand and gratitude in the other and to be stretched large by both."

It's my conviction that moving from conflict to communication will be our next learning curve. In closing this chapter, I hope to leave you a composite of my wisdom and that of others I admire. In *The Art of Loving*, Erich Fromm explains clearly ". . . love is an art." It requires discipline and learning. He tells us "in spite of the deep seated craving for love, almost everything else is considered to be more important than love: success, prestige, money, power – almost all our energy is used for the learning of how to achieve these aims, and almost none to learn the art of loving."

Unless we move from conflict to communication, beyond bulging belligerence we will find the wiliest ways to slam and throw our toys across the room. *When people feel frustrated, furious or hurt, we strike out or stonewall instead of leaning into crucial conversations. We recoil. It's like trying to hold a voracious, enraged, hot and horny crocodile on a leash.* This is why so many people work in teams when the blast of bullying or enraged eruptions hit the wall. There are times when one facilitator needs the support of another. At an impasse or during gridlock, we shelter each other from the storm and help one another hold onto hope.

I had a client months ago who was so out of control, his rage and words were spurting like blood from his mouth. Every tool I had failed. I sat there, in defeat as I was just writing this section of the book. He was too flooded with anger to hear what I suggested. I grabbed a hold of my "eye" statement and leaned forward, saying, "I hear your intention is to work this through. But I think another therapist may be a better match. I'm getting too old and too tired to sit with non-stop blaming. I can't help you unless you listen too. I understand you may need to unfurl some of this for a while, but I suggest you ask for a counselor who can sit with it indefinitely."

It brought up the question: Is teaching communication enough? Can conversations really cure? What if untold psychosis from multi-generational trauma is too steep a hill to climb? There will always be exceptions, people too deeply wounded to heal. But that is not my emphasis here. Still, sincere and respectful dialogue along with guardrails for safety does heal most people.

With counselors who have done this work in themselves and trained well we can accomplish it. Authentic, caring counselors too.

When people have assurance of keeping our *dignity during dialogue*, we will want more of it. I see that what moves sessions, in *compacted conflict* – towards reconciliation – it's when each person becomes real. *Reunion requires revealing ourselves.* Leaders need to do this as well. If we aren't capable of vulnerability, we won't be capable of compassion. Counselors need to be trained but also provide a safe environment for people to open up.

My main message is: *don't shut down or lash out.* It disempowers our collective circulatory system. Keep communicating. I saw the satisfaction from "doing it" with a couple I worked with this week. They ended their sessions, ready to go on without me. He said he hated leaving because it was his favorite time in the week. The guy loved being in therapy! Like sex, we want more of it if it's good! It's a huge relief when we feel heard with respect. "When denial is no longer necessary to protect us from the pain of our experiences in a punitive society, individuals, and the nation, too, will have access to that energy for creatively solving problems." (Milburn, Conrad)

She perceived asking for what she wanted as nagging.

They were a good example of what works. First, they identified their *intention* in therapy. (You have to know your aim.) They wanted more ease in living together. They explored, without interrupting each other, what might be at the bottom of their upsets. She was angry about not having enough support with house chores. He was

144

miserable around her tense, rude demeanor. He actually wanted to be more helpful to her. She shut down out of fear of attacking him verbally. So, she wasn't asking for what she wanted. What was under her anger? In her history were generations of women who were caretakers, always in charge of families, patronized with no support. The apple doesn't fall from the tree. She felt taken for granted, like her mother before her. At the end of the session I asked if anything helped them. *Admitting he was on egg shells and wanting to please her was new information to her.* When she shared why she was so uptight it was because *she didn't want to hurt him* – he was surprised. She perceived asking for what she wanted as aggressive and nagging. She really didn't *want* to poke him with a stick! Her tears brought them both empathy instead of stiff necks. New understanding unfolded as they got under the usual blame cycle. You never know what's hidden underneath that rock. This is just one short story out of thousands of lives in turmoil.

We've convinced ourselves not to work through differences. Why bother? Pick your battles. Those people are too difficult anyway.

So, can this kind of communication happen everywhere? Who would wake up in the morning and say, "I guess I'll enter a conflict today?" You're right. Without ensured safety, we are scared to be open. You can't force a garden to grow – it's impossible. Still, we can create conditions, for it to flourish. *There has to be an agreement on how it is done*, on the infrastructure and willingness to do social and emotional learning.

Civil conversations connect us. We're naturally afraid of conflict. But, there is inevitable deadness if we *don't do it*. As one of my clients uttered at the beginning of a couples session, "it feels dangerous." And it does. How do we know that someone won't yank off the Band-Aid? James Baldwin put it well: **"I imagine one of the reasons people cling to their hates so stubbornly is because they sense, once hate is gone they will be forced to deal with pain."** (*The Fire Next Time.*) We are afraid it will embarrass us or be too painful if we deep dive. But, it is the opposite.

Here's the problem: we're at an impasse in our human evolution. We've convinced ourselves not to work through differences. Why bother? Pick your battles. *Those people are too difficult anyway.* Action is more important, not talking about it! We stay busy railing at leaders, husbands, bosses, wrongful wars, military mistakes or police brutality . . . much of this is valid, but there is little realization that the crime is also happening inside and between us. Our biological tendencies to attack or withdraw are so deep seated, going back through ancient history and the cave man.

Taking responsibility for our own avoidance of conflict is essential. And, a safe scaffolding is crucial. Bessel Van Der Kolk explains: "trauma occurs when one loses the sense of having a place to retreat within or outside of oneself to deal with frightening emotions or experiences. This results in a state of helplessness . . . a feeling that one's actions have no bearing on the outcome of one's life." (*The Body Keeps the Score*)

We are afraid we will feel embarrassed. So, we remain even a mystery to ourselves. We're at an urgent turning point in our civilization. If we are to thrive – communication is the key. Without that, all the solar roofs and financial assistance we muster will eventually fail. Without cooperation we can't survive. As Patten writes: "A great transition is inevitable, either to a life-sustaining society or to a gritty, diminished human future." He elaborates, "The only way we can come to terms with the many dimensions of our ecological crisis- and with all of our built in resistance to acknowledging and acting upon it – is to become a conscious, effective, connected community, and act together."

We can only move from our present state of self-protection and stubborn self-importance toward cooperation by bowing to our vulnerability. *But, resistance to opening ourselves is a worthy opponent.* We are embedded in a culture of defenses and debate – what I call the *court of law.* Blame flails from us, like "YOU said, YOU didn't, why did YOU?" These discussions are circular and wearing. I see families arrive to counseling emotionally thread bare – like shredded tires.

Still, every important endeavor hits a phase of despair and grit work! Shadow work isn't easy. Try getting rid of one on a sunny day. Even our leaders are buckling, like the wonderful New Zealand former prime-minister, Jacinda Ardern, who accomplished gun control there. She retired this year. Caroline Lucas, a recognized member of Parliament in Britain is leaving Westminster as I write this. Her values invigorated our toxic world with concern for animals, glyphosate and teachers funding. There's grief as the columnist comments on it: "With a forlorn sense that politics isn't working and that democracy is broken . . . she is standing down with her vision of meaningful change." (Neal Lawson, opinion / *The Guardian* 6/8/2023)

Our globe is teetering on a pivotal axis. Yet, invention is also rising out of ashes, such as Brazil's President Lula attempting a "peace coalition" with a group of countries sitting at the negotiating table.

Other facilitators are working hard to improve communication during entrenched conflict. The Bridging Divides initiative from Princeton displays hundreds of mediators trained for conflict in communities in the United States alone. (**BDI@Princeton.edu**) Places like Costa Rica are known for their commitment to peace and nonviolent conflict resolution. It abolished its military in 1949. Switzerland is renowned for its policy of armed neutrality and hosting international negotiations. Canada has a history of using diplomatic channels to address international conflicts. There are other organizations emerging in this endeavor worldwide.

> *Joanna Macy captures the cure: "Everyone at some level feels distress over the worlds future, then we all have a lot to say to each other – once we break through the fears and taboos that keep us silent, indeed, it is often in the act of expressing our deepest concerns, that we discover what we feel and know. Furthermore, in the process of communicating, then, change occurs: new ideas and new visions arise."*
> (Despair and Personal Power in the Nuclear Age)

I've learned lessons from life, leaders, and clients who are on the side of wisdom. One of the most stirring stories for me, in this conclusion, includes the work of Kathy Kelly. Her ability to move from conflict to communication is demonstrated by her brave work. She brings dialogue across divides to places such as Afghanistan, Yemen, and Gaza. At the beginning of the ghastly aerial attacks pounding Iraq, in March of 2003, Kathy and her team labored long days visiting hospital wards where maimed children moaned, trying to recover from surgeries. In spite of being arrested more than sixty times, she continues in her calling. She wrote, "I remember sitting on a bench outside of an emergency room. Next to me, a woman convulsed in sobs asking, "How will I tell him? What will I say?" She needed to inform her nephew, currently in emergency surgery, that he had lost both arms and she was now his sole surviving relative. A U.S. bomb had hit Ali Abbas's family as they shared a lunch outside their home. A surgeon later reported that he had already told Ali that they amputated both of his arms. "'But," Ali asked him, "will I always be this way?" Kelly wrote: "I returned to the Al-Fanar Hotel that evening feeling overwhelmed by anger and shame. Alone in my room, I pounded my pillow, tearfully murmuring, "Will we always be this way?"' (Common Dreams, 3/14/2023, *Blood Does Not Wash Away Blood*, Kathy Kelly)

The question remains: Can we move from conflict to communication? Will we wake up in time to repair our own dissonance?

As we weave together, in increasing numbers, we'll knit our societal fabric back together. There's an urgency for a new narrative, away from ego and individuality – "Customer service," wellbeing for all, not just the top few, and education that enables communication.

Larger numbers of facilitators for dialogue across divides are working internationally now including the Carter Center "infusing a new morality:" Switzerland is known for its role in international negotiations. Costa Rica has a commitment to peace. Braver Angels continuing conversations between people with different political views, Sylvia Haskvitz, Certified Trainer and Assessor with the Center for Nonviolent Communication, and others are working throughout the world for peace. Richard Harwood, *Stepping Forward*, is opening conversations with communities. Men Against Violence is offering effective peer led groups. Bohm Inspired Dialogue with Linda Ellinor, co-author, *Dialogue: Rediscover the Transforming Power of Conversation*, Susan Campbell's work *Getting Real*, Harville and Helen Hunt-Hendrix are now working internationally with families, couples and groups – and the list is growing. Edwin Rutsch founded the Center for Building a Culture of Empathy. There are many more conflict trainings including Diana Leafe Christian's work with distressing conflict in communities internationally. (Beatrix Austin's Overview of Approaches and Resources, Head of Dept. Conflict Transformation Research, Berlin.) Lasting peace between Egypt and Israel accomplished in 1977 at Camp David Accords. (Jimmy Carter and Anwar Sedat.) Speaker Peter Coleman, along with his book, *A Way Out,* encourages a movement, the joining of many organizations doing conflict mediation.

I think therapy and communication is like putting a puzzle together. Each piece of ourselves and our history eventually forms a clear picture of who we are and who we want to be. Sometimes it's overwhelming seeing all those fragments.

Then, "Oh My God. There it is!" We discover the whole picture – our new selves and better relationships.

Teaching conflict resolution in the schools will enable youth to grow up understanding *what makes us hate and how to heal it.* As we value communication and cooperation more, learn how to use our anger to solve problems skillfully, then we will knit our global sweater back together.

Dialogue comes from the Greek words "dia" and "logos," essentially "meaning flowing through." In contrast, discussion comes from the Latin word "discuss," meaning "percussion" and "concussion" – to shake or "smash apart." Communication comes from the Greek translation "to share."

We can flip the idea that blame and bullying are power and instead assert that communication is more fun and credible. Then we can enjoy connection and conversation. It can seem messy at first, but inevitably it builds a nest for us to rest.

The belief that Godzilla's anger, with its huge tail bashing, throwing its weight around, pounding the ground, tossing, crushing buildings and living beings is an outdated definition of power. This archaic image of heroism is deadening. We cling to this old, overblown model. It's in our tribal bones. *We are inundated with images of strength and aggression through media, Hollywood, news, politics and pictures.* Even the holocaust was highly motivated by radio waves and negative narratives. It is embedded in us – *the*

Here's the problem: we've convinced ourselves not to work through differences.

Why bother? Pick your battles. Those people are too difficult anyway.

strong man, the big guy is in our DNA. He is our rescuer, even while he's selfish, disappears with another lover, beats the kids or kicks the dog.

David Brooks portrays our present backward behavior: "To be moral in this world, you don't have to feed the hungry or sit with the widow. You just have to be liberal or conservative, you just have to feel properly enraged at the people you find contemptible." (*How to Know a Person.*) The glorification of toughness has been passed on for generations. Can we now imagine a new story? Building momentum away from conflict toward communication.

As Michael A. Milburn and Sheree D. Conrad elaborate, in *Raised to Rage*, there are psychological roots to our aggressive politics. "Individuals who reported higher levels of physical punishment as children were significantly higher in anger." They add, "Because of its potential for abuse, parental discipline may produce negative emotions in some individuals and teach them lessons about the misuse of power."

We are hitting a crescendo of cruelty. We've ostracized "the other" long enough. Many of us are ready for a new kind of Earth. In 2003, some 10 million people demonstrated against the United States impending invasion of Iraq. By many accounts at the time it was the largest single day of anti-war protest in history. More than a million people jammed London's center, while huge "throngs marched in Rome, Berlin, Paris, Barcelona, Madrid, and Sydney. In New York City, hundreds of thousands braved the bitter cold to rally against the war. 'The world says no to war' was the slogan and the reality." (David Cortright 2/24/2023 *The Impact of Anti War*)

Positive change happens with an idea. Among the lessons that I've learned from life, good intention can move mountains. Notice how cars on the road manage in the thousands each day, they're full of all kinds of people – on medications, insomniacs, kids chewing on ice cream bars, screaming couples, but somehow we keep the flow going at a high rate of success.

In closure, I'm pushing us all to do more radical reaching out to heal divides. Let's face it, much of our civilization has diminished the idea of dialogue, the bedrock of democracy. We judge "open conversation" as a nice idea, reserved for "softies," for liberals who get nothing done but "talk" about it and we argue that psychotherapy is dwelling on the past. The purpose of counseling is not to ruminate on the past (a common argument) but to seek what's at the root of our rage, frustrations and despair and redirect our lives to new choices.

Our prejudices harden us. They block our interest in differences, our regard for variations, like the way we stare at art.

In small ways, we need to lean in toward daily communicating skillfully, ensuring that our kids know how. In larger ways, my ask of us is to value good communication, learning it in the schools – and understanding what's at the bottom of it, historically, emotionally and genetically.

Tich Nhat Hanh once articulated: "We live in a time when there are so many sophisticated means for communication: email, telephone, fax, yet it is very difficult for individuals, groups, and nations to communicate with each other. We feel we *can't use our words* to speak and so we use bombs to communicate with each other." We boomers in the 60's knew in our bones "Everybody look what's going on . . . nobody's right, if everybody's wrong." (Buffalo Springfield, *For What It's Worth*)

A resurgence of tyrannical leaders around the globe is a sign of our pressing need to reckon with our collective shadow. "If we are to flourish and prosper, we need to understand that our urgent and necessary task is to transcend and dismantle our narcissism, both individual and collective." (Elizabeth Mika, M, LCPC, *Gifted Resources of Northern Illinois*.) A lack of empathy and a sense of entitlement is intrinsic in narcissism.

We have to know the diagnosis before we name the cure. So, what is slowing down our progress? There's a tenacious, clingy fixative gumming up the process of useful dialogue – like crazy glue. I could see it in myself too. When I was triggered or upset – my own ability to self-regulate, to manage or even comprehend the meaning of my emotions wasn't easy. What they call "agency" flew out the window. If I was fragile or tired – I recoiled from people, spewed criticisms or told myself negative stories about them.

Collective curiosity is handcuffed by our fight or flight impulses. Prejudices harden us. They block our interest in differences, our regard for variations, like the way we stare at art. Society inhibits exploration.

Also, architecture and design for conversation separate us. The speaker is up front, probably above, and there we sit, being told, not heard. "If political activism only means going to boring public meetings and venting your anger after having waited a long time for your turn, most people aren't going to want to be involved." (Patten, *A New Republic of the Heart*)

As Linda Hill, Harvard business school professor elaborated the new task is to: "create the space where everybody's slices of genius can be unleashed and harnessed and turned into collective genius." (3/13/2015 Ted Talk)

Imagine more communication everywhere, including employers replacing "job reviews" with conversations – revealing needs on both sides, corporations co-owned and decisions made between us. The new, needed paradigm is horizontal power (shared among people, like different organs of the body or a system.) Even the department of motor vehicles would encourage input from the public about how they regulate exams and rules, etc.! Our towns would meet with police consistently, military, health care practitioners with citizens, etc. Speakers at conferences would divide their time equally between audience comments AS WELL as questions. All meetings would exist on one level of flooring in the round. As Ella Baker, Civil Rights Activist, declared, "Rather than someone with a fancy title standing at a podium speaking for or to the people, group-centered leaders are at the center of many concentric circles. They strengthen the group,　forge consensus and negotiate a way forward."

Just pretend for a moment – you're way up above the earth, looking down – from a bird's eye view. You see us all running around, gunning each other down, squabbling over parking places. You fly over people being flooded or dying of hunger while others are bloated, on diets or living in gated castles. Seriously, this is crazy! I don't want you to think a good argument isn't helpful sometimes, even blame might need to burst our seams. These should be done by agreement. But, this book is about the necessity of negotiation, intimacy, disclosure, and community building.

We don't realize – the heroes are us.

I see the potency of healing everyday. Sometimes I try to explain to friends how my day was, being a psychotherapist. How do I portray the unportrayable? The potential of people in genuine dialogue is moving and exciting. I say, it's like sitting in the front row of a panoramic movie theater watching a wild whitewater rafting trip on the wide screen. The gushing water is tipping and ripping the boat apart. And I am supposed to be the one with a life raft! Then I slow the pace down and the river flows again. Chaotic, deep currents crashing against the boat, obstacles and rocks move aside and adrenaline subsides. People don't realize what conflict resolution work is like and what's possible for our earth – in contrast to the chaos and pain in the news.

As I turn the corner on this book, I see a world in turmoil and I'm afraid. Lessons I've learned the hard way from home to the therapy office, from media to the news, reinforce my message. Violence, greed and fighting needs to stop. It is my conviction that conversations can change the world. I believe that as much of the globe speeds and flails its way to the end of democracy – the work of listening and communication will walk us out of conflict.

In Nazi Germany, there were too many secrets, too little circulation of information, not enough questioning. There is power in numbers if we coalesce, in conversation.

Naomi Klein writes it well, "The point is to make our way out of this collective vertigo and get somewhere distinctly better together." I agree with her. (*Doppelganger*)

Our gnarled-up emotional hairballs congest our bodies and the body of the earth. The more we do radical reaching out, the more interconnected and empowered we'll be. It's an effort in a world that habituates us to turn inward and toward technology. It will take extending ourselves, but it's essential to communicate our way to world peace.

On your deathbed, will you have remorse about not having completion in a lost relationship? If you haven't risked the conversation for closure, regret is what you'll get.

Is closure possible? Maybe, but not always - remorse and empty holes take more than a lifetime to heal. But, frayed endings can be knitted back, making reconciliation relieving, helping us and our world become more whole.

Yet, if you have the courage to communicate, here's what's possible: people sharing the wealth, talking to each other and enjoying teamwork. Imagine humans exchanging ideas and labor – laughing, being authentic, having affordable counseling, shaking hands after a job well done. As Catherine Price says, "True fun is a special confluence of playfulness, connection, and flow." I say, connection comes from communication. We could all look like bees cross-pollinating, buzzing in conversation, and understanding each other. Imagine. We, the people, you and I, creating this new way, from conflict to communication – everywhere.

As I turn the corner on this book, the theme here has been constancy and communication, building trustworthy relationships and our own ability to connect respectfully. When we do we'll have real faith. When our political leaders become bound to negotiate - not free to kill - we will know peace. As Jonathon Haidt warns in *The Anxious Generation*, phone free schools may help. Human health calls for community.

Now, let's look at the tools for crucial conversations. Here's your diagram for easy recall in conflict. It's in your face.

"HOW TO SAVE FACE"

Cliff Notes for Communication

- **INTENTION** – Use your FIRST Eye – I statement explains your intention (aim or hoped for outcome in our conversation)

- **SECOND** "I" – Eye – I feel is for stating personal, heartfelt feelings here . . . usually fear or hurt, not anger

- **MOUTH** – Use your wishes and requests / this is where anger gets directed. Your anger is best used for asking for what you want or wish for

- **EARS** – Listen deeply and mirror back what you heard

"I" statements help us move from judgments, criticisms and blame to our own beliefs, fears or longings. For instance, if you think modesty is better than wearing revealing clothing - that is your value. Our needs can be valid, our ways to thrive, survive, or barriers to connection. As Marshall Rosenberg wrote: "Our repertoire of words for calling people names is often larger than our vocabulary of words to clearly describe our emotional states." (*Nonviolent Communication*)

FROM CONFLICT TO CONVERSATION

More Instruction Booklet on HOW TO DO IT

Communication for Couples, Partners, or People in Groups of Conflict

I've learned lessons from watching what helps clients in conflict. These instructions are simplified because in combat we are anxious and disorganized. **There are essentially only two parts to the process that I use. The first is attentive listening. The second is making requests and wishes.**

First, decide together when a good time to talk might be.

This can be done in groups with family, friends or with couples:

***Decide* to each take 5 to 10 minutes while the other person just *LISTENS* . . .**

- The first person shares what they feel and need.
- Stay with "I" statements and away from blame.
- Go into vulnerable feelings

EXAMPLE: I feel hurt or afraid.

The partner **just listens**, mirrors or repeats what they heard – this is terribly important. *NO interrupting, asking questions or defending yourself* – JUST listen (this can't be overstated.

We all instinctively want to interrupt others and defend ourselves. **And repeat the gist of what they said, the underlying feelings that stand out.** Attend to the emotions or gut of what is said. This requires slowing the pace down. My clients insist the slower rhythms ensures being heard.

The speaker is best heard if they talk in shorter spurts so the listener can remember what was communicated.

Hear what they are saying, **not what you are thinking.**

This is critical and hard to do. Once you get good at this you can guess at what you are hearing, but always check with them. *Do not give advice, ask questions or make assumptions.* "I'm guessing that you felt sad when your parents didn't get along with me. Did I get that right?" then ask:

"Is there more?"

This question triggers the brain of the recipient to feel more deeply heard, safer and to experience your sincere listening.

This means letting go of judgments, you are being Sherlock Holmes here. If you *recite or report* what they said, if it is too robot like – they will not feel heard. *It requires you to lean into empathy and deep listening for their feelings.* Even if they can't identify them, you can still listen for them. "It sounds like you felt afraid of rejection when that happened. Did I get that right?"

Acknowledging the details puts you back in the weeds.

When you reflect what you've heard you're listening for the message. When you just report, you sound like, "I hear you saying that I did not pick up the baby's milk." Reporting details can trigger conflict, "NO, I did pick up the milk, just later than you wanted . . . etc."

Details rather than feelings drops you back into debate. *Mirror back to them the feeling you hear, "I'm hearing you say you were hurt when I forgot to pick up the baby's milk." Just reciting facts can put you back in circular arguments, "the court of law."*

The EYE is MOST essential. ("I" is for individuation)

When you hear "YOU" – it's an exploding gun. *Do not use the word YOU unless you are mirroring, "what I hear you saying is . . . "*

Take turns hearing each other. Repeat above with other partner speaking:

One person states their REQUEST of the other (their wishes for change).

It's ideal if it's doable. If the partner cannot do it, they can ask for another wish. Maybe something like: "I wish we could cuddle more on weekends" or "I wish you would return my texts sooner" or "find a way to work through conflict." It is your wish and, if it is not an attack, you can use the word *you*. The wish gives us a way to express anger in a constructive manner. "When partners unconsciously protect each other from aggressions they numb the relationship." (Galit Atlas, Ph.D., *Emotional Inheritance*)

Asking for what we need isn't always easy. The fear of feeling "undeserving" can loom large. Yet, embracing this act can foster a sense of worthiness in ourselves. Additionally, it provides an opportunity for growth within our relationships with partners or family.

Then the next person does the same and receives mirroring – being heard.

You can experiment with these guidelines a bit but the essential thing is that you hear each other without criticism. It's imperative to slow down so the other person feels heard. Take time after the above to relax, or get out and take a break or do something soothing together or do more dialogue if you want that. Research shows that walking helps the brain absorb and calm down during contentious conflict so some of my clients even do what we call, "walk and talk."

I suggest not asking questions

Questions can feel like you're back in court again, being cross-examined – "Why did you do so and so . . . ?" **Questions can feel like an interrogation and be a way to escape your own vulnerability.** They are wonderful socially, especially an open-ended question. My favorite one is, **"What's on your mind these days?"**

If you absolutely have to ask a question, preface it with "I need to understand" . . . etc. Questions can be used with great care because they can put people on the defensive. Questions are used too often as an inquisition, not an inquiry.

Behind every question is a statement – make those instead, offer a context first. So, instead of "why do you always show up late?" Try "I worry when you are late" or "I wonder about how eating a lot of sugar effects you. I've been worried about it."

In conflict, stay away from questions. But, while socializing, Charles Duhigg insists, in his book *Super Communicators*, deep questions can create closeness like "What do you regret most?" or "What would be your perfect day?"

Listening with genuine curiosity is the key.

It calms our defenses and the lizard brain and our tendency to demonize. Ideally you can physically lean in . . . toward them and really imagine how THEY ARE FEELING . . . because we are usually wanting to jump ahead with our side of the argument.

Arguing and interrupting does not work. It is "one up." I can't tell you how often I have to gently stop one person from interrupting the other.

Some of this might feel robot-like at first but after a while it builds in a new rhythm. It's like getting in shape physically can feel awful at first, going to an exercise class, then become a positive habit. *These techniques are borrowed in part, with my own slant, from many teachers.*

My purpose here is to make repair happen with simple tools . . . so you can recall them under stress.

When we're angry or flooded with feelings we need easy to remember tools. These are on your face. Two eyes, a mouth and ears.

- The first "Eye" is for intention,
- the second "Eye" for feelings,
- the mouth for wishing,
- and ears for listening.

As we are heard, we ideally go deeper, what I call "down the ladder" of emotional memory.

At the top rung we have obvious perceptions, intellectual beliefs and judgments, as we lower into our gut and heart, vulnerable feelings, past experiences, learned behaviors and beliefs, admitting our old fears – are at the bottom, at the root of our powerful reactions. Peering into your past will offer insight and allow others to see you and get closer to you.

Intimacy is: *into – me-you-see.*

If we don't feel safe, we will want to "save face . . . ." How do we create safety? Listen attentively, don't argue, debate or give advice without asking (another top down attitude . . . . "I know better than you do" . . . .) If you insist, wait until all is complete and then tell them you'd like to offer an opinion with permission.

Margaret Mead said, *"For the human species to evolve, the conversation must deepen."* Still, we remain like little kids in adult bodies throwing mud pies at each other. We are a shame-based culture, so we are either embarrassed by our raw feelings or get shamed by others.

The eye, or "I" statement is more profound that it seems. It matters so much because it forces us to reflect on ourselves instead of focusing on the other person's faults. **Sometimes you can use this phrase, "the story in my head is" to explain your fears or judgments.** Paradoxically, "I" creates more connection than using words like "we" or "you." *This is harder than it sounds because it's unfamiliar.*

What we are actually doing in this process is wondering, "what is under there?" As Alice Miller wrote, "For the majority of sensitive people, the true self remains deeply and thoroughly hidden. But how can you love something you do not know, something that has never been loved? So it is that many a gifted person lives without any notion of his or her true self. Such people are enamored of an idealized, conforming, false self." (*Drama of The Gifted Child*)

Over half of marriages end in divorce – they could be passing on cooperation instead to their children.

Inquiring into our own inner recesses, what is the history behind our fears and wants? Why are they so sensitive to us? Was I pushed around as a kid, fired from my last job, told to stand in the back of the line in the military? When was I ignored, forgotten, or smothered? And much of our memory may be out of reach, not recalled, but trust me, if you have strong reactions – they come from the past as well as the present.

Using "I" diffuses the compulsion to stare at the other person's faults. It helps us reflect inward instead of pointing fingers. You can't have connection with two or more attacking selves. "You" is an affront. It's like two hard boards clapping against each other. (The word "we" can be used in less contentious, kinder, more sociable situations.)

In my therapy practice, I stare at stressed faces glaring at each other at an impasse – at their wall. Partners or families usually start with a presenting problem, like money, sex, addictions, etc. **Often, I tell them that the issue doesn't matter so much to me, (unless it does harm)** – *my concern is how are they talking about it?*

We dread conversation about "the relationship," even with co-workers and neighbors. Yet, with a dab of discovery, instead of debate, and a few simple tools, relationships and partnerships revive.

Even, in our homes, "the hub of the wheel," imagine the ripple effect if that was a place of open conversation, a sandbox for discovery, tranquility and vibrant life – generation after generation.

Approximately 62 million married couples exist in the U.S at this time. There are 7.8 billion people on the globe. Even if a small proportion of those learned skilled communication, we'd have a new world. Over half of marriages end in divorce – they could be passing on to their children cooperation instead. We can move from conflict to communication, personally and politically.

ACKNOWLEDGMENTS

In boundless appreciation to the people who have devotedly worked on this topic themselves, through talks, interviews and writing. Without saying, in endless gratitude to my clients who gave me their entire insides with devoted trust. And to you who edited, toiled with me and listened to my emotional hairballs throughout this process, especially deeply listening to me and getting your hands on the text: Jane Whitsett, Linda Ellinor, Sylvia Haskvitz, Raymond Baltar, Steve Klein, David Brigode, Thomas Shetka. And to the magnificent magician Suzanne Parrott, editor, designer and friend.

ABOUT THE AUTHOR

Katy Byrne, LMFT, MA, has been a licensed psychotherapist in California for over forty years and a columnist for The Sonoma Sun and Women's Voices for twenty years. She is the author of *The Courage to Speak Up*, *The Power of Being Heard*, and *From Conflict to Communication (Lessons from Life and My Therapy Office.)*

Katy hosted radio at KSVY in Sonoma, California, and KVON in Napa for fifteen years. Her passion for helping clients, combined with her rolling words, moves us to laugh, cry, and speak up. Her fervent view of change and how it happens, both personally and politically, gets us off the couch. Her audacious authenticity stirs her stories, blending theories and ideas from many great thinkers, authors, and activists.

Katy Byrne's mission is clear: We urgently need to create a world bolstered by communication—not conflict. And she shows us how.

Katy Byrne, LMFT, MA
ConversationsWithKaty.com

Mom and I devotedly treasured talking about books

How I adored
my Dad. He
thoroughly
enjoyed being
a barber for
53 years of his
working life.

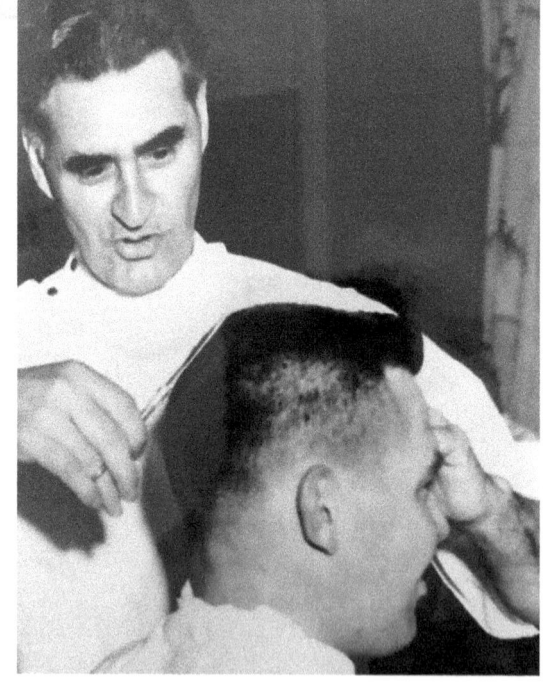

I was so in love with my husband.
But, love isn't enough.

Laughing with my beloved brother
when he was at his best.

Einstein, teaching me to write -
getting out my emotional hairballs.

Katy - 1951

I popped out of the womb fully infused with multi-generational lessons about life from past generations.

Me - these days.